T0276323

STORIES
FROM THE
STOOP

STORIES
FROM THE
STOOP

A MEMOIR OF THE 1960s BRONX

STEVE BERNSTEIN

Skyhorse Publishing

Copyright © 2017, 2023 by Steve Bernstein
First Skyhorse Publishing edition 2023

All rights reserved. No part of this book may be reproduced in any manner without the express written consent of the publisher, except in the case of brief excerpts in critical reviews or articles. All inquiries should be addressed to Skyhorse Publishing, 307 West 36th Street, 11th Floor, New York, NY 10018.

Skyhorse Publishing books may be purchased in bulk at special discounts for sales promotion, corporate gifts, fund-raising, or educational purposes. Special editions can also be created to specifications. For details, contact the Special Sales Department, Skyhorse Publishing, 307 West 36th Street, 11th Floor, New York, NY 10018 or info@skyhorsepublishing.com.

Skyhorse® and Skyhorse Publishing® are registered trademarks of Skyhorse Publishing, Inc.®, a Delaware corporation.

Visit our website at www.skyhorsepublishing.com.

10 9 8 7 6 5 4 3 2 1

Library of Congress Cataloging-in-Publication Data is available on file.

Jacket design by Brian Peterson
Jacket photo credit: Getty Images

Print ISBN: 978-1-5107-5996-1
Ebook ISBN: 978-1-5107-6136-0

Printed in the Untied States of America

TABLE OF CONTENTS

For my sister, Amy, who is in my heart every day. Your last words to me in this life were, "Steve, you have to be happy, I never made it." Ame, I'm working on it.

ACKNOWLEDGMENTS

Thanks to Elaine, my sweetheart from the old neighborhood. After reconnecting forty-five years later, it was our trip to The Bronx in 2015 that inspired me to write this book.

Thank you isn't enough for my best friend, Judy. As only a best friend can, she got to bat cleanup as my toughest and most loving editor.

A heartfelt thanks to my Western Massachusetts writing community along with Writers in Progress, Write Angles, and Pioneer Valley Writers Workshops, who offered relentless critique and constant encouragement.

Teams of professionals helped me polish and market this book. Without Skyhorse Publishing, Archangel Ink, and Full Stop Art, you would likely not be reading these words now.

My fellow faculty at The Care Center in Holyoke, Massachusetts, recognized that *Stories from the Stoop* would appeal to young adult readers and inspire them to tell their own stories. I sure hope so.

How do I thank everyone who helped proofread, critique, promote and, most importantly, encourage me on my writing journey? It's impossible to fully express my profound gratitude to each one of you, but *you* know who you are. All I can say is "I couldn'ta dunnit widout ya!"

INTRODUCTION

"**Is it okay** if I just tell my own story?"

It was 1994. I was forty and, after more than twenty years as a plumber, I decided to get my bachelor's and then my master's in environmental studies. I found myself in a course called "Storytelling" at Antioch University in Keene, New Hampshire. I was with a dozen students, all half my age.

In the first few minutes on the first day of class, each student was asked to describe how they would use storytelling in their environmental work. One after another, they each explained how they hoped to incorporate stories from indigenous cultures from around the world.

That just wasn't me. It didn't feel genuine. Who was I to tell other people's stories? I had my own indigenous stories from the streets in The Bronx where I grew up.

So I asked the professor, "Is it okay if I just tell my own story?"

And that's when the story, "Wolf," was born. For the next twenty years it was a story I told to at-risk teens in my work as a mentor, humane educator, and special education teacher. When I told the story of me and Wolf, the barriers between me and the teens disappeared. The magic of me telling my story gave them permission to tell theirs. And like me they had tough stories of their own bottled up that needed to be told, that needed to be heard.

In 2017, "Wolf" became the first of seven stories in this memoir about growing up in The Bronx in the sixties and seventies. I hope these adventure stories of a tough time, a tough place, but always hopeful and often fun, will inspire you to tell your own stories. When you do, let me know. I want to hear them.

To me, stories are everything.

CHAPTER ONE

WOLF

———

It was late spring, 1968. South Bronx. I was fourteen years old. Sun out, birds chirping, kids playing, people on the street. I was shooting hoops down at the P.S. 90 schoolyard when Karl came running in, all out of breath.

"Gog, they're robbing your brother, man. You better get up there. Now!"

Karl, the neighborhood messenger, was about ten years old, bone skinny, not quite four feet tall, with buck teeth. For some reason, he walked around with a small wooden cane, not with a curved handle, but straight with a little carved African head on the top. Whenever something was going down, Karl was right there, getting into it and mixing it up.

My street name was Gog. I don't remember how I got that name. It just stuck. We had gangs, though not like the ones in inner cities today. Mine was a hanging out, basketball-playing, and girl-watching kind of gang. I was a street kid. No matter what pressures were around me to stay off the street, I kept going back. I needed the gang to survive the inequalities of the street. I was the only white kid. Being in a gang was a little better than not being in a gang. It gave me and to some degree those around me the illusion of credibility.

I dropped the basketball and ran out of the schoolyard through the chain-link fence. I barely heard Marcus, the kid I was playing ball with, yell out, "Yo, Gog, what's a matter? Where you goin'?" I sprinted the two blocks up the hill and around the corner to the courtyard of my building. A kid was using both hands to shove Richard backwards towards the courtyard wall and then with one hand, he tried to reach into the pocket of Richard's pants, looking for money. This kid was bigger and older than my brother. I ran up the steps of my stoop and, without thinking, jumped right in. The kid was standing in front of a chain that served as a fence to separate the cement walkway where they were scuffling and the four feet of dirt that was supposed to be grass leading up to the side of my building.

I pushed the kid, hard. He tumbled backwards over the chain, did a reverse somersault, and hit his head on the brick building. I was strong, always ready to fight or defend, but usually a voice inside of me kept me calm. Not that day. Driven by adrenaline, I pounced. The kid wasn't hurt too bad. He regained his senses, realized he was hurt, and through his bloody tears cried, "I'm gonna get my brother and my boys after you!" I was relieved that I hadn't killed him, and more relieved that he hadn't hurt my little brother.

"Go ahead, get outta here and don't ever bother my brother again!" The kid took off. Within a minute the adrenaline settled down and I realized I was scared.

What if the kid did have a gang? What if he did have an older brother? I had my brother to worry about and no one I could call on to help me. I said I had a gang, but the reality was that I was the wrong color. In my neighborhood, the other kids were all Black and Puerto Rican. There was no way they were going to help me—the only white kid—fight a gang of Black kids. I knew that.

Very calmly, I said to my brother, "Go get Dad." Though I knew Richard would never find him, I was buying time. The truth is my father was either not home or sleeping off a drunk. Any way you sliced it, he was unavailable. My father and brother never talked to each other. When Richard was younger and diagnosed with a brain injury, my father would say, "He can't be a son of mine."

After Richard left, a million panicky thoughts and feelings passed through me. What was I going to do? How would I survive this? These questions and the emotions surrounding them were way too familiar to me.

I could get on the subway and keep on going. That idea lasted about two seconds. *Yeah, you can always run, but you gotta come back sooner or later.* I learned early on living in The Bronx—or maybe it was just living my life in general—*get it, before it gets you.* I suddenly felt so all alone.

Karl the Messenger had witnessed everything. After he came down to the schoolyard to get me, Karl made sure to follow me up to the stoop of my building to watch the action. He took off when the kid did. Karl buzzed around the block and told everybody what was going down. In lawn chairs in front of their stoops or watching from their windows, my neighbors were waiting for the big show. I felt that much more alone when I realized that I was going to be the afternoon's entertainment.

The week before, plastered all over the front page of the *Daily News* was a story about a Jewish couple in their eighties who lived around the corner. They committed suicide together. The suicide note read, "We no longer want to live in a world where every day we get beaten and robbed. We had enough of that in Germany before we came to America." This was big news, a telling commentary on life in The Bronx at the time.

By sending Richard away, I gave myself time to think. I sat down on the stoop alone, looking straight ahead, avoiding the gathering neighbors. Running away was out of the question. I didn't have anybody to ask for help. People on the street wanted a show. Cops did not come to my neighborhood.

Sitting on my stoop, every imaginable fear raced through my mind. My heart was pounding through my chest. My gut ached, and I started to sweat. Time was running out.

Suddenly I had this amazing, almost lighthearted feeling take over. I thought about Wolf and how crazy it was that everyone thought he was vicious. He was this big, I mean really big, Malamute/wolf-type dog that my sister Amy's boyfriend, Mike, brought to my father one day. Mike was a sailor on a boat where they needed a watchdog. Well, Wolf didn't cut it. He basically slept all day. My father ended up with Wolf and used him as a mean-looking deterrent to junkies breaking into his plumbing shop. Before Wolf came along, just about every week somebody broke into his shop and stole his tools and materials. Right behind the cracked storefront window was a shelf where Wolf would lie, looking scary enough that nobody would go near the place. It worked.

Wolf and I hit it off. He was magnificent. Aloof, noble, and so strong and agile, half a step away from the wild. He was by no means lazy with me. A watchdog he was not; he just looked scary. Not to me, though. I loved him and admired him. I wrestled with him and played with him all the time. I was the only one he responded to in a fun way. Everyone else, he more or less ignored.

Though Wolf was unbelievably powerful, he would never even bite the fleas off his back. Except once. We were out jogging one day when a drug dealer sicced his Doberman on Wolf. Even though I could see Wolf didn't want to, in an instant Wolf bit down on the other dog's neck and snapped it, killing him in seconds. I never saw anything like it in my life. I think Wolf knew his life, and maybe mine, were in danger.

I started to talk myself into the fact that Wolf looked ferocious and he would help me in a jam. I had a hard time thinking of Wolf in any way other than as a big puppy. The reality was, I had no other plan.

I unclipped my retractable key chain with about fifteen keys on it from my belt, walked over to the shop which was adjacent to my stoop, opened the padlock, the overhead door lock, raised up the massive steel curtain with the graffiti sprayed all over it, unlocked the two deadbolts on the entry door with the splintered jamb, pushed it open and as cheerfully as I could, yelled out, "Wake up boy, let's go for a walk." He loved when I said that. I put his giant choke collar on, the one with spikes that dug into his neck. I grabbed the chain leash and said, "C'mon boy, let's go!" Wolf woke up, hopped off his shelf, stretched, yawned, and came out with me. So casual, so calm, his tail wagging and that Malamute smile looking up at me, tongue out, eyes bright, thinking we were going for our daily romp around the neighborhood.

I must be nuts, I thought to myself, *Wolf is barely awake*. I ran him up and down the block to liven him up a little. He was all I had in the world to help me survive what I was starting to believe was my last day. I walked back to the stoop with my happy dog and the neighbors watching, eagerly waiting for the show to begin. The dread was agonizing.

As I stood waiting on the sidewalk, I had to hold Wolf's leash tight and pull up hard on his neck with a steady pressure while he sat, glued to my side. My mind was clear. My heart was racing. I blocked out everything around me and stood there, solid, outwardly emotionless in front of my stoop, leaning with my back against the brick column, pulling upward on the leash with all my strength, keeping Wolf sitting upright, the chain wrapped double around my fist, Wolf literally attached at my hip. Both of us frozen, him with his tongue hanging out to the side, his teeth in a snarl, his eyes, one blue, one brown, looking wild and crazy. An image of toughness, real or contrived, maybe a little of both. We waited.

Karl the Messenger came running around the corner. "They coming for you, Gog."

"How many?" I asked.

"About twenty of 'em." I knew he was exaggerating, but I didn't know by how much. The next minute seemed endless. I wanted whatever was going to happen to be over with. I kept myself contained and together to show them that I had nothing to worry about. I convinced myself that Wolf was all I needed. He was all I had.

They came around the corner and started crossing the street to my stoop. There was one real tall, older guy in front of this pack of younger guys all carrying sticks, bats, and chains. One guy had an old umbrella he was going to whack me with. The older guy, maybe nineteen or twenty, came right up to me while the others surrounded me, obviously the leader of the pack. The guys followed him, looked to him for cues. I kept an eye on him, and an eye on them, and figured that if he gave the word, they would jump me and beat the shit out of me. The leader was like any other guy in the neighborhood—cocky, walked with a prance, at the ready for a fight, all attitude. Exactly the kind of guy I avoided.

This guy was lean and wiry, about three inches taller than me. He had scars on his forehead and a look that told me he came up hard, harder than me. All this in an instant. Registered, noticed, taking it in. I blocked out my fear, the fear that should have been exponentially higher than the regular day-to-day fear I felt just walking down the street as a target. A moving target. A target that was gaining a reputation of not backing down.

I stood fast and tall, gripping Wolf's chain as hard as I could. I glanced down out of the corner of my eye and saw Wolf, right there, eyes bulging, frozen to my side, in a snarl. This was it! This was all I had. I thought, *Let's get on with it, man. I'm so tired of being scared.*

The big guy came up to me, looked me up and down with hate in his eyes, and said, "What the fuck did you do that to my little brother for, man?"

I picked my head up, stared directly into his eyes and said, in as controlled a voice as I could muster, still pulling up on Wolf, him growling now, "He was pushing my

8

brother and was gonna' take his money. I had to protect him."

"You so much bigger and older, you shouldn'ta hurt him so bad."

"Your brother's sixteen," I said. "I'm fourteen. I didn't mean to hurt him."

All the while we were talking, I was alert and watching what was happening around me. It was like a slow-motion movie. The big brother was standing three feet in front of me, and the rest of the gang formed a circle surrounding us. Could it be true? Were they afraid of Wolf? He was right there, like a clamp on my side. He had no choice since I was almost strangling him. They didn't realize that if I let go of the leash, he'd drop down and go to sleep. Or would he? I made it look like he was chomping at the bit. Was it me making him look vicious? Or, was Wolf protecting me?

The big brother said, "You a lucky motherfucker that you got your dog, man, or you'd be dead meat." I showed no sign of the relief I felt. I gave a kind of nod in agreement. He said, "Some day you not gonna have that mutt with you. You better look both ways at every corner, cause I'm gonna' get you, man."

I didn't care. That's some other day. Though my face showed no emotion, on the inside I was praying that they would just walk away. Now.

The big brother turned to leave and his boys gathered up and followed him. When he got to the corner, he stopped, turned and looked back at me. I stared right into his eyes. I was still motionless standing there with Wolf at my side. I know it's strange, but being who I was I couldn't help but think that he wasn't going to get me; he needed to put up a front. After all, he too was a big brother. I think maybe he understood. I never saw him again, but I did look both ways at corners for a while.

A few minutes later, Karl came around the corner and said, "Don't worry, Gog, they're gone." I waited about three more minutes and then let loose on the leash. I took a deep breath. Me and Wolf collapsed on my stoop. I glanced up the block. The spectators were packing up, going about their business as usual. The show was over.

I started petting my friend, thanking him as I stroked his fur. He was already relaxing and didn't seem to remember or care about what had just happened. How I wished I could be like him. I gave him a real nice walk and some soup bones and let him back into the shop.

Richard came out after everything was over and said, "I couldn't find him." Puzzled, I looked up. I was now calm, relieved, adrenaline settling down, sad and somewhat reflective, sitting on my stoop.

I asked, "Who couldn't you find?"

He answered, "Dad. You told me to go find Dad, remember?" Richard had missed the whole thing. Maybe he hadn't bothered searching.

I told him, "Oh, yeah, well that's okay. I'm all set now."

When I got home that night, my father was still sleeping off a drunk from the night before. Just four flights up from my stoop in our apartment, he had been in bed all day. I had this fleeting thought, *Wow!* He was there all the time and could have helped me! But then that thought was instantaneously replaced with the familiar feeling that there's nobody I can count on when I'm in trouble. Except, now, for Wolf.

During that summer, I played with Wolf all the time. I took him to the Botanical Garden up near the Bronx Zoo where he could run and splash through ponds and streams, just like in the country. Boy, did he love to run! I was so taken with him. He gave me hope that anything was possible.

It was a long walk to the Botanical Garden. Miles of concrete and cars and noise and people and stench and smog. In this magical place, there were trees and animals other than pigeons. The air even seemed cleaner. It was the place we escaped to, just our own clean and green paradise. That's where we both came alive and felt free. Me and Wolf fell in love.

I started high school that fall. Over the summer, I had gotten into the habit of playing with Wolf every day. So in the fall after school, after basketball practice, and after my messenger job downtown, I would stop in to give him a good run and some soup bones. He loved to chew those bones down to the marrow.

One October night I got home late from my job downtown, around 8:00 or 8:30. It was dark, cold, foggy, and drizzling. My street was dead. No cars, no people, only the double-parked plumbing vans out in front of the shop. There was that unmistakable wet, NYC, ozone, dog shit odor in the air.

And there was Jimmy, this creep that my father had working for him, standing outside the shop. The graffiti covered overhead steel door was halfway rolled up.

As usual his presence put me on edge. Jimmy was leaning against the storefront of my dad's plumbing shop, drinking Colt 45 out of a brown paper bag, an unfiltered cigarette dangling out of the corner of his mouth. His lips formed a smug grin, barely hiding his rotten, brown teeth.

I never understood why my dad kept him around for so many years. He was in the habit of stealing my dad's tools and then selling them to junkies who usually sold them right back to my dad. And, he'd still have his job the next day. Jimmy was my dad's drinking and whoring buddy. One time, he tried to get me to do some heroin. Another time, he was fooling around with a woman in the back of the shop and told me to join in.

I hated Jimmy. And he knew it. Although I was only fourteen, I let him know to stay the fuck away from me.

Just behind him, the front door of the shop was propped open with a wooden chair. Inside, the fluorescent ceiling lights were glaring. I could see old meat hooks still hanging from the ceiling. The worn and stained butcher block counter had been converted to a workbench with a pipe vise on one end. Wrenches, black steel pipes, pipe fittings, and liquor bottles scattered all over. The door of the walk-in meat freezer, where all the valuable plumbing tools were locked up, was wide open. The stink of rotten meat still present. Towards the back of the shop, I could see my old man snoring on a makeshift bed, an empty bottle of Chivas Regal dangling from his hand off the side of the cot.

I knew this shop all too well. After school and on the weekends my job was cleaning up and rearranging the mess from the previous week's work.

Behind Jimmy, was the broken plate glass window and the shelf where Wolf slept. I couldn't see him. Only the leash and collar were on the shelf. His empty food and water bowls on the floor. No Wolf.

I screamed, "Where's Wolf?"

Jimmy was all too eager to answer, knowing how much I loved that dog. With a smirk, he said, "He's gone, man."

My fists and teeth clenched. "What do you mean, gone? Where the fuck is he? What did you do with him?" I was frantic. I almost reached into my pocket to get my knife. I wanted to slit his throat. Because I knew.

"I didn't do nothin'. It was your daddy," he said with a smile. "Yeah, he got good and drunk, and lost your dog in a card game."

It felt like a kick to the stomach. I ran wildly, crazy with fear and rage, all over the neighborhood, in the alleys, in basements, up and down the block, down in the schoolyard. No Wolf.

I went upstairs to the apartment and collapsed. The house was dark. I didn't cry. I do now.

CHAPTER TWO

SKY KING

When I was nine and my sister Amy was twelve, my mom sat us down in our living room, which also served as the dinette and our parents' bedroom, and announced, "I can no longer be your mother."

She was baking our favorite cookies, oatmeal with raisins. It must have been a Saturday because all my favorite TV shows were on. I had just gotten my cowboy outfit off the top of my dresser, where I kept it handy so I could easily jump into action when my shows came on. I had my straw-colored felt cowboy hat, a light blue shirt with mother of pearl snaps on the flap pockets, a silver pistol, a badge, and a holster. Pants didn't seem to matter; I wore my pajamas. It was the getup I'd wear if I was watching *Sky King* or *Roy Rogers* or *The Lone Ranger*.

When the Yankees were on I had my baseball glove, my cap embroidered with an NY, and a number 7 pinstriped jersey from my Little League team just like Mickey Mantle. That outfit stayed folded under the cowboy outfit on top of my dresser, ready to go when there was a game on. It was the same jersey I wore when I hit that grand slam that summer for my team, the only hit I got all season. Afterwards, my dad took me to the father and son Little League breakfast. That was the only time either parent came with me to a Little League event.

The aroma of the cookies made me feel warm and content, but also sad. The only times we had cookies or ice cream or candy or anything like that was when there was something bad going on like the drunken, vicious tirade the night before. My mom used sweets like my dad used booze.

Me and Amy were watching *Sky King*, our favorite show, about a sheriff who flew around in his plane, the Songbird, catching bad guys with his niece, Penny, and nephew, Clipper. The show was a modern-day western, a cowboy in a plane.

We were living in the projects up on University Avenue, kind of West Bronx, kind of South Bronx. It was 1963 and I was nine, Amy was twelve, and Richard was six. The rickety, staticky, rabbit-eared, glass tube TV sat on a metal folding table in the living room of our tiny four-room, thirteenth-floor apartment.

As usual, my old man was nowhere to be found. When he wasn't nowhere, he was home in a drunken rage yelling, screaming, bemoaning his existence, and scaring the shit out of all of us. Just like he had done the night before. His alcoholism was advancing and more often than not, he was gone many nights during the week. My mom worked mostly emergency room night shifts as a nurse in Morrissania Hospital.

Richard wasn't in the living room at that moment. Maybe he was in our bedroom building or demolishing something, hard to remember exactly. He was somewhere in the apartment because otherwise me or Amy would be with him outside.

I suppose when most people hear the word "projects" or "The Bronx," some scary, inner city images may arise. It wasn't like that. Not yet. It became dangerous, as did most of the neighborhoods of The Bronx, especially the South Bronx, as racial tension of the sixties exponentially intensified and heroin became an epidemic.

Richard was born with a different kind of brain operating system than most people have. Back then they called it "retarded." I remember terms like *premature baby*, *oxygen deprivation*, and *brain injury*. Today, it probably would be called Asperger's, autism, something on some spectrum, whatever. Or, perhaps another label like PTSD from a traumatic childhood. He was different. If he wasn't stressed out or depressed by having to conform most of the time, you could tell he had his own peaceful way about him. He was content alone and found millions of ways to entertain himself. He made things out of odds and ends, played with toy trucks and never spoke ill of anybody. Tinkertoys were really his favorite past-time. He created the most elaborate contraptions with those little colored pegs and round wooden blocks with holes. Spaceships and buses and trucks were his preferred inventions.

The time I remember Richard the happiest is when we spent summers way upstate near the Canadian border where my mom's dad owned a junkyard. He would play hours on end with greasy gadgets and be in his own world in old rusted out jalopies, trucks, and school buses. My grampa had a secretary, Dorothy, who was possibly also his girlfriend. The summer I was nine, my grampa gave Dorothy's teenage son, Irving, an old car to fix up. The car didn't run and the roof had been torn off. After Irv got it running, he taught me how to drive it, using only first gear, which was fine because I never went over five miles an hour. Every day I took Richard out for our daily junkyard adventures, a big grin on his face.

When Richard did talk, he talked mostly to himself and made funny squeaking noises with his teeth. He had no friends. He had to be prodded and nagged just to get up in the morning and get dressed and go to school. Understandably, his outer world oppressed him. Kids at school, kids in the projects bullied him or worse—shunned him.

When my dad was home, he took it upon himself to crack the nut. The nut being Richard's defiance and stubbornness which continuously confounded my dad.

Richard would hardly ever bend or give in. And if he did, it would be kicking and screaming.

In my dad's eyes, Richard was imperfect and, worse yet, nearly impossible to dominate. One Saturday in the Junior High School 82 schoolyard, my dad, drunk as usual, actually renounced Richard as his son. After three hours of nagging and badgering, my dad failed to figure out a way to teach Richard how to ride his bike. He was crying and bleeding from a fall, but kept getting back on that bike. It was torture, not only for my brother, and I guess in a way, for my dad, but for me as well. I watched and winced and kept quiet, hoping for the best. My dad finally threw up his arms and announced, "I'm done with you, you are not my son." He left the schoolyard fuming. Richard, got off the bike, kicked the tire, and collapsed on the cement next to his fallen bicycle and cried. After a few minutes, I convinced him to give me a try. He was riding on his own in less than an hour.

* * *

Friday night, the day before my mother's Saturday morning declaration, the scariest drunken tantrum to date occurred. Like I said, my dad was drinking more and more. That night he came home drunk, yelling, waking up neighbors, probably the whole building, banging on the door until I had to let him in.

STORIES FROM THE STOOP

So, try to visualize a fourteen-story building, one of seven in the projects, eight apartments on each floor, us on the thirteenth floor, down on the end of the hallway. Four little rooms, three little kids, no mom at home, and then the banging and the wailing and the yelling and the screaming and the cursing somewhere around one in the morning. Try to imagine not just the fear in us kids, but by then the shame of it all. No other dads acted like this. Up until that point, when the drunkenness wasn't so obvious, loud or violent, all I had to do is lie to my friends when they asked how come your dad is never around? I told them that he was a special kind of secret agent and was away a lot. I remember one day, when he was sleeping, I stole his badge from his Bronx building inspector job, and flashed it to my buddies, proving that he was some kind of cop.

I unbolted the apartment door locks and sprinted back down the hallway to the bedroom I shared with my brother who was hiding under the covers in the bottom bunk of our bed. I caught a glimpse of Amy straight ahead in her room, scuttling under her bed like a scared little animal running for cover. My dad stormed into the apartment and raced down the hallway, screaming and cursing and banging on our doors, but he didn't come in. I heard a loud crashing, almost cracking noise like a giant tree breaking in two right at the moment my mom came home.

* * *

From the time I was about five, wherever my father would go, he took me along. According to my mom and the aunts and uncles who still chose to associate with us, Amy had been the apple of my father's eye. Well, that stopped and I became the chosen one. I not only was shown off at the building department office and on the job sites, I was also taken to bars and whorehouses and at times left with people, places, and things no kid should ever see. Crazy as it might sound, I loved it. It was exciting to be a little kid, shown off by his dad, seeing things that no other kids saw.

I remember being dropped off for a few hours at a woman's apartment, plunked down on a sofa and given a Coke. She told me, "Now, you be a good boy and wait for your daddy to come back." I think it was Harlem, she was Black, very nice to me, and even though I was only about six or seven, I thought she was beautiful. She had an Afro, was tall, her skin was like cocoa, a beautiful round face and sparkly white teeth. Thinking back, she probably was younger than twenty years old. She spoke with an accent. I didn't know it at the time, but it was a Southern accent.

As my dad opened the apartment door to leave, she said, "Don't worry Mistah Hy. I'll take good care of your boy." And then with a smile and a wink she added, "In a few years, bring him back and I'll make a man out of him."

I drank my Coke and watched as every half hour a man came into the apartment, gave me a strange look, went with this beautiful woman to the bedroom, came out and not fifteen minutes later, the same thing would happen all over again with another man.

Now, don't think for a second that I was abused or hurt or beaten in any way. No. In my view, there was nothing and I mean nothing more fun or exciting than going on adventures with my dad. At least, up until that Friday night when he came home scaring us, screaming, breaking things, and shaming our family.

I remember being left in bars countless times, drinking Cokes and waiting while my dad either went to a backroom with a wad of cash or left for an hour or two. Other times he was gone all day and into the night. Now, that was an education! The bartenders, the waitresses, the patrons, all different colors, men, women, they all liked me. They looked out for me and kept the Cokes coming as they were told to do and paid to do by my dad. He would buy round after round of booze, all night long wherever we went. When I was eight, the Cokes switched to Tab because I was getting to be a fat kid with cavities. So, you see my dad really was on top of things and doing a good job taking care of me. At least the best he could or knew how to do.

Before you walked into the bars, you could smell the beer and the hard liquor and I swear, sometimes, I got drunk just by breathing the air. I don't remember a lot of drugs, maybe some pot, mostly drinking, drunkenness, noise, and smoke. Lots of smoke. Smoke clouds, smoke rings, smoke coming out of mouths and noses. Smoke hovering near the ceiling, catching the light just right.

I got my entertainment by watching people, better than any TV show or movie, in my opinion. I would play games like pinball, and other times some of the cooler guys would teach me eight ball, if there were pool tables.

If the bar was in a white neighborhood, the patrons were older white guys who mostly sat and drank and smoked and stared off. Or, they became hostile and threw chairs and glasses around and walked out not paying their bill. Some of the women were just as scary as the men.

If it was a Black neighborhood, there was music and laughing and dancing and pool tables and good looking women. I'm not sure if the Black customers were younger, but the Black bars were more lively and fun to be in.

Very rarely were the bars mixed. I liked watching people and trying to figure out what the big deal was. What the big attraction was of drinking booze and smoking cigarettes. Either it made the white guys mellow or the Black guys energized. I liked the Black bars best.

Whatever the neighborhood, the wooden floors were sprinkled with sawdust and the surface of the bar itself was bowling alley hard and shiny. When I'd sit on the tall barstools, my sneakers dangled below me way off the floor. I couldn't lean my elbows on the bar like the adults and I had to tilt the glass of soda to meet my mouth. I drank so much soda, and wouldn't get picked up for hours that I almost peed in my pants. I never wanted to go use the dark and smelly bathrooms, so I just held it.

When I was eight or nine, my dad's drinking was starting to escalate, and at times we didn't see him for weeks. Come Christmastime, or any holiday really, he went on benders for days on end. Christmas to New Year's was the worst. You might think, well if he wasn't home being crazy drunk, isn't that a good thing? Well, we were used to his drinking. So, in the beginning, when his drinking was somewhat predictable, we predicted. We predicted how life was going to be. We predicted how we couldn't bring friends over. We predicted how to lay low. We predicted how to time eating meals or watching TV or sitting at the table doing homework to avoid him coming home. The verbal abuse turned physical. Prediction turned into projection, worry, fear, stress, and angst.

My mom was no match for the loudness, threats, and the verbal and emotional abuse, but she provided us kids with a sense of protection and stability just by being there. When she told me and Amy she had to stop being our mother because she had to work nights and home-school my brother, we started to fend for ourselves.

Sometimes my mom wasn't around for long periods of time, weeks into months, because she had to go way up north, almost to the Canadian border, to look after her father who had a bad heart. Though she was one of four siblings, it was my mom who took charge of his care. Her older sister lived in Brooklyn and was also a nurse.

Her younger sister lived in Montreal not fifty miles away from my grandfather and her brother lived in New Jersey. All of them had resources, intact families, businesses or good jobs, yet it was my mom who lived in the projects in The Bronx, not two nickels to rub together, who took Richard and left her other two children behind in the hands of a madman.

Here's what me and Amy witnessed while my mom was gone: Chairs were thrown. Bottles, plates, and glasses were smashed. Crazy characters came in and out of the apartment. Bo was this guy with totally white hair, short like a crew cut, yellowish skin, no teeth and intense, clear blue eyes who walked around with a bucket and sponges and bottles of cleaner and a chamois. He lived in the streets and made his living washing cars. When my old man was drinking, Bo would seek him out for five bucks to wash his car and share some booze.

Every day, drinking, drinking, drinking. Smoke, haze, laughing, crazies. Sometimes Amy got groped. Sometimes I lashed out and dumped booze down the sink and screamed at the top of my lungs for everybody to clear out. Sometimes it worked.

Just before leaving on one of those trips upstate, my mom went to my bedroom closet to get her checkered fabric suitcase from the top shelf. I walked into my room and saw her placing her suitcase on the floor. Her other hand was on the window handle, pushing the window open. She was crying. The windows were metal frames and opened out, two windows per frame. They opened out like doors would open, taller rather than wider. It was winter so the windows were closed. Living up on the thirteenth floor, it always seemed to me that if somebody really wanted to jump, it would be easy. There were no screens or bars or anything that would hinder someone jumping.

At night, after bad things happened in the apartment, I would go to my room, look out the window, watch University Avenue way down below, bleary-eyed from the tears, all the little cars and their skewed headlights and taillights zooming back and forth and the even smaller people and think to myself, *What would it be like to just jump? What it would be like to get my desk chair, move it up to the cast iron radiator under the window, step up, open the window and walk out?* Nope. Not in the cards. I needed to stay put and do my job.

I went over to my mom and put my hand on her hand which was resting on the window handle. Now, I don't have any idea if she was thinking of jumping. I wasn't sure. She seemed startled. I asked, begged, pleaded with her to take us away, get us out of here. Leave him. With tears in her eyes she sighed, "I have to go take care of Grampa, so take care of things while I'm gone. Look out for your sister."

When my mom was helping her dad, Amy and I often didn't have enough food in the house. My dad would come home on any given night drunk, yank us out of bed, and take us to a restaurant for dinner. I remember one time we were taken to Arthur Avenue, the Italian mafia section of The Bronx, just off Fordham Road where my old man had a lot of business dealings. He took us to his favorite place, Mary's, and ordered the owner to stay open and cook.

Somewhere around midnight, Amy and I were forced to eat raw clams, mussels, spaghetti and meatballs until we got sick. The food kept coming and coming and my father kept screaming at us, "Eat! Eat!" The owner seemed like a sweet, meek guy who was upset and nervous about the whole thing. He kept saying, "Hy! Hy! Stop doin' this! Stop making your kids sick. Don't make me do this!" He must have been afraid of my father, otherwise a restaurant owner wouldn't do this crazy thing my father was ordering him to do.

It seemed to me that my father had something over a lot of people. They did what he told them to do. From a stool in any one of the dark and smoky bar rooms, Arthur Avenue was the neighborhood where I often witnessed my dad's world unfold just like the wad of cash unfolded out of his pocket. I always wondered where all that money was coming from and going to in that hardly any of it went to my mom or us. It seemed to me like way too much money was in and out of my dad's hands for us to have to live in a project, with crappy furniture.

It was one of those times when my mom was away taking care of my grampa that my dad cracked up his car by hitting an elevated train column supporting the Third Avenue El. My old man was one of the first Americans to buy the newly designed Saab 96 in 1960. It was a sporty kind of fastback made by an airplane company. When he cracked it up, he was drunk and left the scene. He forgot I was in the backseat.

At any given time, Hamsky, my old man's childhood buddy from the Lower East Side, would make his way north, seeking out my dad for a few bucks and maybe a good night's sleep with a roof. Hamsky never recovered after the war and ended up on the street. My dad sometimes would take out Ham's army discharge papers from a locked metal box, showing me how he was a war hero and got honorably discharged with a medal of honor. Sometimes my dad would cry when he showed me the papers.

My dad was a war hero also. At least, that's how he told it. He was a bomber pilot. He flew B-17s. The name of his plane was The Myassis Dragon and, just in case you didn't get it, underneath was the translation: My Ass is Draggin'. It had a picture of a colorful, comical dragon on the fuselage, back towards the tail end of the plane.

My dad showed me black and white aerial photos of the German factories and cities he bombed, along with a photo he took of soldiers helping concentration camp survivors at the end of the war. Times like that would bring tears to his eyes. That's when he told me about my uncles. At least, up until then I thought they were my uncles. They were my dad's cousins who were concentration camp survivors. They didn't speak much English and always seemed serious. They had numbers tattooed on their arms. I think they were German or Polish. Thinking back, I believe my dad, like his friend Ham, also never recovered from the war.

He used to tell me stories about his squadron where there were all kinds of guys from all over the place. As he recalled there were Jews from New York, Indians from out west, the Irish guys, the Italian guys, cowboys, all Americans, all fighting to defeat Hitler.

He told me how he loved England where he was stationed, the countryside and its people. He often talked about how he would fly the B-17s from England over Germany and how sometimes he would fly hungover or even drunk. He said everybody did. One day he showed me a photo of his squadron and named most of the guys, wondering where they were and what happened to them. He pointed to a few who didn't make it. Quite a few. The black and white photo was from 1943. My dad was twenty-one years old.

For most of my childhood, if my dad took a day off from drinking, it didn't mean he was sober. It just meant he was hung over. He was either hungover or drunk. When he was drunk and our mom was out of town, our apartment was a revolving door of other drunks, crazies, whores, and street people. If my dad wasn't drinking, I would come home to a different dad and a different kind of house guest, people like Louis Armstrong, Count Basie, and Ella Fitzgerald. Puccini and Bach. Rodgers and Hammerstein and sometimes *The Man of La Mancha* made an appearance. Leonard Bernstein was a permanent resident. I always wondered if we were related.

If my dad wasn't communing with this eclectic group of friends through his beloved recordings, he would be in deep reflection with other friends, not through music but through the written word. Friends such as Nietzsche, the philosopher, and Shakyamuni, the original Buddha. A big part of the time me and Amy spent with my dad, we were forced to listen to his "sober" rantings, his philosophical views as if we were fellow theologists and as if we cared. Amy acted like she cared so much more than I did. These smoky one-way rants lasted for hours and went on for decades.

When the music was playing in the living room, it was loud. My dad would be slouching on the folded-up sofa bed, a thin flimsy metal frame with blue foam cushions, not a couch, like other people had. He would be chain smoking, laying back, lost in sound and reverie.

My dad's thirty-three and a third LP record albums were always meticulously organized in wire racks. The records, in their white sleeves and colorful jackets, were stacked cover side up. The wire racks sat on a large wooden plank, anchored into the plaster walls with heavy metal angle brackets. Next to the records sat the Emerson stereo receiver and turntable, all kept pristine under an opaque white plastic cover, to keep the equipment free of dust and cigarette ashes. The gigantic AR-2 speakers sat on the floor on either side of the shelf. God help you if you messed with that system. The books, hundreds of them, sat on the upper shelves. All philosophy and religion. No kids' books. Ever.

* * *

Back to that Friday night when my dad tried to bang down the apartment door. Thankfully, my mom did come home right after I let my dad in. Somebody had called Artie, the project cop, because of all the racket. It wasn't the first time. He calmed my dad down and then left after a few minutes. All that night I heard yelling and dishes crashing, my mother whimpering. Sometime around dawn things quieted down.

During the night, I snuck out of my room, assuring both Amy and Richard we would be okay. I listened to my mom and dad's conversation, such as it was. I planted myself in the hallway behind the wall that separated the entryway of the apartment from the living area. I could hear them but they couldn't see me. I crouched down and realized I was in a pile of plaster chunks and blue paint chips, next to the pricey Heywood-Wakefield maple armchair my mother had bought the year before with her own money, trying to dress our place up a little. The chair had three good legs and the fourth leg was splintered.

The rest of the fourth leg was stuck in a hole in the hard plaster wall. That was the crashing, cracking noise we had heard when my dad first came home.

My dad was accusing my mom of wanting too much, spending too much, and, more than anything else, for ruining his life by bringing the burden of children into it. He blamed her for tricking him into having children and ruining his chances at finishing his apprenticeship as a diamond setter downtown and forcing him to get a city job. She gave no backtalk. She knew better. I think it was the first time I got a glimpse of how tortured and pathetic and sad my parents really were.

When my dad was ranting about how terrible his life was, having this gigantic burden of a family, I got confused because I remembered a few snapshots of Amy from before I was born. Didn't seem to be many, if any, photos taken after I was born. My mom later told me she didn't take photos because she wanted to remember only the good times. I remembered Amy, maybe two years old, laughing, happy, smiling, space between her front teeth, pigtails, beautiful, cute, bubbly. She was running into my dad's outstretched arms, him kneeling down and also smiling at her. I remembered another photo, about the same vintage, maybe that same day, where my dad was relaxed, stretched out reading a book on a lawn and Amy was sitting on his chest playing with some leaves. Happy. When I heard him say how terrible his life was now, it confused me. Something big must have changed since those photos were taken because he and Amy both looked like they were happy and loved each other. A lot.

* * *

When Amy was around ten, she started pulling out her hair. Sometimes she would have next to no eyebrows or eyelashes. Sometimes she pulled hair out of her head and ended up with bald spots. It worried and confused me to see my sister doing this to herself. I didn't know how to help her or how to deal with it.

Right around this time, my dad signed both he and Amy up for night classes at Roosevelt High School up on Fordham Road. Every Tuesday night, for a month or two, he would take Amy to a calculus class. I remember Amy coming home and telling me how stupid it was. She complained that she had no clue what they were talking about and felt out of place and there were no kids in the class. She knew our dad wanted to show the world what a genius she was for an eleven-year old, and so to make him happy, she went. He made her raise her hand and answer questions that he gave her the answer to. He took her for ice cream after. According to Amy, that was the best part.

* * *

After my mom sat me and Amy down and told us she could no longer be our mother, she explained why. She had to focus her time on taking care of, teaching, and protecting Richard, in addition to working. Believe it or not, it was a relief, to me at least. I agreed with her. Me and Amy needed to care for ourselves and together we would look after Richard. I always felt guilty that I had it better than Richard. I did all I could to be both brother and father to my brother, and I know I fell short.

I was no longer compelled to hope for parenting that she could not provide. This new arrangement was better than that constant rejection. So, me at nine and Amy at twelve were orphaned and became parents all at once. Looking back, this was the moment when my mother succumbed to the insanity that my father's condition and behaviors imposed. This was the moment that my mother stepped over the line. She was unable to put her children, all her children, first, above her fear, denial of reality, and infatuation with her insane husband. Of course, I didn't consciously realize it back then, but that was the moment I was forced to discount her as my parent.

I had an inept mother and a crazy father. I not only was orphaned and instantaneously made a parent to my brother, I also had another charge: my mother, my child-like mother.

After her one-way, one-minute announcement, my mom returned to the kitchen to finish baking the cookies. Me and Amy looked at each other, shrugged, and then went back to watching TV. *Roy Rogers* was on next which was good because I still had my cowboy getup on and Amy loved Dale Evans, Roy's wife. She was not only beautiful, but she often helped Roy catch the bad guys. Amy liked that.

It felt to me like I was on a vacation after that talk. A weight was lifted. Amy, on the other hand, had a worried expression on her face. She watched Roy Rogers and Dale Evans and pulled out her hair.

Right then on that Saturday morning, the apartment was peaceful, my dad wasn't around, and oatmeal cookies with raisins were on the way. The day after the talk, Sunday, two days after the crazy drunk banging down the door nightmare, I changed. It's not like at nine years old I had this epiphany or this articulate conversation with myself about how life was going to be different. No. It's not like me and Amy strategized on our new family roles and relationship with each other. No.

It wasn't about what I said or thought. It was more about what I did. I took my cowboy outfit, my baseball jersey, and my gun, holster, and badge off the top of the dresser. I neatly folded them up and stashed them away behind some pants and shirts way in the back of the big bottom drawer.

CHAPTER THREE

ORDER ON THE COURT

Isaac was a kid I met one warm September Sunday afternoon in the P.S. 104 schoolyard in 1966. I was twelve and he was fifteen. He changed my life, and, one time even saved my life. Isaac taught me about the jump shot as well as how not to get jumped in the street.

I learned way too young about hate and racism, but I'm glad I did. My friendship with Isaac taught me that people are basically the same, regardless of skin color. I saw up close the scary, sad, and terrifying lengths people go to when they are pushed too far and become desperate.

The Bronx was burning. Crumbling and exploding. And I'm not only talking about the buildings. Its spirit was dying. Its people were scared, angry, worried all the time, people of color and whites alike.

I had all I could do to keep myself and siblings safe, get to school and try to make sense of the constant chaos on the street. The fights, the muggings, the junkies, the racial tension. I'm not sure which was worse: what was going on in the street or in my apartment. I'm not sure which was worse: my dad's alcoholism, insanity, violence, and irresponsibility or my mother's denial of it all. Both were a bitch. But Isaac made it all okay. Better than okay—I had a friend.

That Sunday in the P.S. 104 schoolyard, as usual, I kept to myself. I was practicing pitching with my Pennsylvania Pinkie ball. Nobody else was in the schoolyard until this tall, lanky Black kid came in dribbling a basketball. He started shooting on the crooked, leaning, all metal, rusted basketball hoop.

It's funny how when you love the sport, you get used to shooting on anything: garbage cans, milk crates, even fire escape ladders, which you can pull down to whatever height you need and just jam through them. You seldom found a good hoop back then in The Bronx.

This kid was intently shooting jumpers. When he missed a jumper, he'd throw in an occasional layup and then maybe a dozen foul shots. It was a routine, a drill he must have learned somewhere. He sure made it look easy and fun. He was so tall that when he rebounded, he almost got rim.

Stealthily, or so I thought, I stole a couple glances at this kid playing basketball as I continued pitching against the wall, about forty feet away. His hoop and my wall were sandwiched in between the two wings of P.S. 104, not easily visible from the street.

Once in a while, he shot a look over at me, too. After about twenty minutes of each of us playing our solitary games, this kid stopped playing and yelled over to me, "Hey, you wanna shoot some hoops ova here?" I didn't want to yell back and announce that I didn't know the first thing about basketball, so I grabbed my Pennsylvania Pinkie and walked over.

It's not like I never had a friend of color; I actually had nothing but. White kids were all but gone by the time I was growing up in this part of The Bronx. But, he was three years older than me, so it seemed strange that he even gave me the time of day.

"So," he said, "Whaddya think?"

"About what?"

"Playin'? Playin' ball with me?"

My spirits soared. The turmoil on the street and the tension at home melted away. He appeared good natured and friendly. I wasn't sure why he paid me any attention at all. It made no sense. Why me? A little non-basketball playing white kid?

Isaac had a softness about him that felt comforting. His words were kind like, "It seems like you got a good arm, the way I saw you pitch," or "I didn't mean to bother you, but seeing as how we're both alone, I thought we could shoot some hoops together."

I said, "Sure. Let's play ball. Teach me." And so he did. I felt hopeful and warmed. I felt playful like the kid I was never allowed to be.

Isaac showed me how to dribble with one hand, not two. Every time he told me to shift to the other hand, I tended to do what's called double dribble, dribble with two hands. Not allowed in basketball, he warned. He was much more patient with me than I ever was with myself. Soon, I was dribbling back and forth with both right and left and soon enough between my legs and then, the ultimate, behind my back. Next came the jump shot. It's not exactly rocket science but at the same time it takes a lot of coordination and skill to smoothly, from the tips of your toes to the tips of your fingers, create this perfect arc, all in one fluid motion and then follow through with a smooth release that all but guides the ball through that metal hoop, ten feet off the ground, as you leap into the air. A hoop that soon became my obsession, my reason to live, second only to this newfound friendship.

After a month of Sundays, Isaac told me we were ready. *Ready for what?* I didn't have a clue. At that point I didn't know Isaac off the court. In fact, when we finished playing each time, he told me to wait five minutes after he left the schoolyard before I could leave. When I asked why we couldn't walk down the street together, he said three reasons: "One, it's not good for you, two, it's not good for me, and three, the world isn't ready for us yet, but it will be." The conversation went no further and, like with everything else in my new friendship, I didn't question it. He knew stuff I didn't. I had so much to learn from him. And most importantly this friendship was the best thing that ever happened to me. I wasn't going screw it up by asking too many questions.

On that fourth Sunday, we moved from drills to learning our plays. Each play had its own number and was written down on a piece of loose leaf paper that Isaac kept folded up in the front pocket of his jeans. The smudged paper was covered with diagrams and arrows. Isaac would call out each play to me:

Play Number One:
- Go under
- Point to rim
- Get pass
- Backwards overhead to Steve
- Baseline jumper

Play Number Two:
- Fake baseline play
- Jump under rim
- Get pass
- Lay in

That next Sunday, Isaac walked me home and met my family, and then I walked him home and I met his. Something shifted. Something good. Up until that point, I had thought Isaac was ashamed to be seen with me. It made sense. A little white kid in a tough, mostly Black neighborhood, tagging along with a guy who had to maintain his image, his coolness, his Blackness. I got it. I wasn't thinking through all of the ramifications of what this friendship looked like from the outside. Maybe our friendship was dangerous for both of us. He risked ridicule and I risked getting my butt kicked or worse.

Other than Isaac and basketball, my life was JHS 82, odd jobs, a weekend job working for my dad, taking care of my brother, chores, and oh yes, Hebrew school. For some crazy reason, it was important for my parents to send me to Hebrew school. Even at twelve, I denounced my religion. Or, at least I thought I did. It wasn't Judaism that I was denouncing. It was the confusing difference between all the other Jewish families and my family. Jews were law abiding. My dad wasn't. I never saw drunken Jews, abusive Jews, or irresponsible Jews. But that's what I lived with. I'm not saying these kinds of Jews didn't exist, I just never saw them. So, Hebrew school? Me? Yeah, right. I did it to make my mother happy.

My bar mitzvah was coming up and I needed to learn Hebrew. My Hebrew school teacher was incredulous that I could be Amy's brother. Amy's name in Hebrew was Channa and everyone thought Channa was perfect. The perfect student, the perfectly behaved young woman. Then I came along. I was disruptive, rude, and picked fights. With everybody. I didn't want to be there. I didn't fit in. In my mind, I wasn't even white, let alone Jewish.

Granted, 82 put all us Jewish kids in the same class, the "smart" class. I'm not sure if it was because we were so smart. I certainly didn't think I was. Maybe we were put in the same class because we were white. And since most of the white kids were Jewish, there you have it. For example, in sixth grade I was in class 6-E3. E for what? Not sure. Enrichment? Excellence? The E classes were almost all white kids. E students skipped eighth grade and started high school in the tenth instead of the ninth grade.

The rest of the sixth grade, all four hundred students went from the level 6–1 all the way to 6–22. Outside of the E classes, 6–1 was for the regular "smart" kids. As the class numbers got higher, skin color got darker. Same for all the other grades. Segregation, New York style.

Walking the noisy, sometimes violent, halls of 82 as a white, Jewish, E class student, skipping a whole grade, meant I had a target on my back. I was the minority. So, I became the tough white kid. I couldn't relate to the softness and the safety of the loving, caring, responsible Jewish families, so I went the other way: rebellious and angry. A fighter. That tough guy reputation made life even rougher for me. Between the fights with the Black and Puerto Rican kids looking to knock me down a few pegs and the frequent requests by the weaker Jewish kids for protection, I was busy.

I was a fighter in 82 and in Hebrew school. Wherever I was, I was an outsider. I didn't belong. One night at Hebrew school, the principal, who was the rabbi as well, came to my class and in a very polite, but no-nonsense way, told me to come to his office. We sat down in Rabbi Cohen's tiny, cluttered office and from behind his desk, in a soft yet firm voice, he told me that he had heard about my disrespectful behaviors in Mrs. Teitlebaum's class. He told me how fond he was of my sister Amy and what a fabulous young woman she was. On that we agreed. He also, ever so casually, mentioned that he knew about my family, especially my dad. I totally appreciated the respectful and kind way that he presented that personal information, information that I was so ashamed of. Rabbi Cohen didn't exactly come out and say he knew my dad was an abusive drunk. What he did say was that although my behavior was bad, he understood.

Rabbi Cohen offered me a deal: he personally would teach me Hebrew and help me prepare for my bar mitzvah, but one-on-one at his apartment, not at Hebrew school with the other teachers and students. I respected this man and so wanted to please my mom so I took the deal. Oh yeah, the other thing running through my mind was Susan, the rabbi's daughter. I hoped that just maybe I could get a glimpse of her now and then. The rabbi and I shook on it and the next week we started.

I was diligent, studious, well-behaved, and respectful. I learned Hebrew and I learned the part of the Torah that I was going to recite on my bar mitzvah day. I so enjoyed learning my part of the Torah that I even practiced on my own at home. According to the rabbi, I was the best bar mitzvah boy he had ever trained.

Rabbi Cohen instilled pride in me and through his teaching, he made me realize what a good religion we had going for us. I found comfort and a sense of security spending time with him. I felt clearheaded around him. He never chastised or belittled me. I was not used to being treated so well. In my house, it was yelling, flying furniture, and endless criticism.

My bar mitzvah training was more than learning Hebrew and Jewish history; Rabbi Cohen offered a model of manhood that was foreign to me, a combination of respectfulness, firmness, and tough love. Rabbi Cohen showed me a side of being a man that I will carry with me forever: the compassionate side. I admired him and hoped that one day I could be a man like him.

After meeting twice a week for two months in the small living room of Rabbi Cohen's apartment, one Tuesday evening in February, Mrs. Cohen came in with a plate of almond cookies and offered me another deal. She said, "On Thursday night after your lesson, if you are a gentleman, you can have tea and cookies with our daughter, Susan." Rabbi Cohen piped in, "I'll be watching you, Bernstein."

* * *

Isaac lived on Nelson Avenue, which was the toughest street in the neighborhood. Many of the buildings were abandoned, windows and doors boarded up. Sometimes you'd see people still living in these dark and shuttered buildings with no utilities, buying time until they got kicked out or arrested.

Like much of the South Bronx, Nelson Avenue pretty much saw its last white families leave by the mid-sixties just as Black families were moving up from a segregated and bigoted South. When they got to places like Nelson Avenue, you better believe they let everyone know this turf was theirs.

Isaac lived in a small two-bedroom apartment with his family: his two younger sisters, his two younger brothers, his mom and, from what I could tell, two fathers. According to Isaac, neither of them were his. His mom asked me to call her Ma. She was skinny and seemed sickly as did Isaac's baby brothers. His two sisters, Yvonne and Yvette, were cute, funny, and always teasing me. I let them.

From the first time I met Isaac's family, I felt welcomed and special. I ate with them several times a week and Ma often invited me to stay overnight. I slept on the floor on a mattress in the kids' room. I felt safer in Isaac's house than at home. The collard greens and the grits took some getting used to, but I loved the pigs' feet and pork chops right away. I had all I could do to keep what I was eating a secret from Rabbi Cohen. I truly believe he would have called off my bar mitzvah and kicked me out of the religion had he known what I was eating at Isaac's.

Every Sunday, me and Isaac practiced our basketball plays at P.S. 104. We were indeed an unlikely but dynamic duo. And that's precisely what allowed us to launch Isaac's business venture that October. Isaac, with his savvy business acumen, come to find out, had had a plan for us all along. Those secret Sunday practices at P.S. 104 were the preparation to get us and the world ready for our debut.

We started making money. It was a different kind of money than I made after school delivering meat for the kosher butcher shop on Featherbed Lane. It was different than the kind of money I made with my father. It wasn't exactly work or a regular job. And no, it wasn't drugs which were rampant. It was basketball.

It all became clear to me soon after Isaac taught me the plays and deemed it acceptable for us to be seen in the world together. The tall, cool Black kid and the little white kid were going to go out and challenge, or I should say hustle, boys on the court, because no way would anybody ever think we got game. Well, hustle we did. He handled the bets and the money and I executed the same basic three or four plays he had taught me. Sure enough we became two-on-two champions. Until of course they figured us out. When that happened, we moved on to another park or schoolyard.

This is how it went down. I'd be dribbling up near the key, Isaac would crisscross around the baseline and under the basket, I would make like I was taking it to the hoop, and Isaac would know to stop dead under the basket. When he did that, I would hit him with a jump pass as he ally-ooped the ball in for an easy two. The very next play would look exactly the same, except, in mid-air when he caught my pass, Isaac wouldn't lay it in. Instead, he would make a ninety-degree mid-air turn so his back faced me, and at the same time he would hit me with a no-look-over-the-head pass to where I was now waiting on the baseline for a nothing-but-net jumper. No nets of course. These two plays and variations of them would easily take us to a record of about eight in ten wins.

Of course, we weren't playing with the cream of the crop. Isaac would carefully pick the schoolyards and judge the level of competition and, I might add, gullibility, well before game time. That's why he made the big bucks. An average take-home from the basketball hustle would easily be ten bucks a week. I got two. I was happy. I would have done it for nothing.

When the weather cooperated, and we weren't in school or on our other jobs, we hustled. Kids on the street got wise to us and started to turn real mean towards me when Isaac wasn't around. It wasn't pretty. I didn't tell Isaac about half of the beatdowns. They were minor. A punch here, a kick there. I stomached it.

It was good to have a friend to show me the ropes. That first Sunday in September when I had met Isaac, my family had just moved out of the projects. We had been living in our new neighborhood for less than a month. I hadn't known a soul.

We moved to 174th Street just off of Featherbed Lane. Even though we had only moved six blocks east of the projects, it was my first taste of street life, mainly because in the projects, there were no streets. The projects were cloistered from the surrounding neighborhoods. Seven buildings, fourteen stories high, eight apartments to each floor, five thousand people. The tall red brick buildings were surrounded by chain-link fences and stone walls on all sides. The project had a cop, a maintenance department, a nursery school, a library, a community center, and about five playgrounds. A city unto itself.

For the first eleven years of my life, we had lived in a four-room apartment on the thirteenth floor. Apartments in the projects were cold, box shaped, hard plaster, and metal. Sterile and dull. As were the buildings themselves.

But the new apartment on 174th Street was in a real neighborhood, a beautiful one at that. Short, six-story brick buildings built in the 1920s and thirties, so different from the identical, modern, nondescript fourteen-story Housing Authority buildings. The buildings in the new neighborhood had character and style. Real architectural masterpieces. The Bronx was famous for its fabulous, lavish buildings.

Unlike the confinement of the projects, the new neighborhood had stores. On Featherbed Lane alone you could find John's Bargain Store, Sandy's Toy Store, Eddie's Shoe Store, Willy's Haberdashery, Freddy's Barbershop, Izzy's Candy Store & Soda Fountain, Steve's Pizzeria,

Chin's Chinese Restaurant, Daitch Shopwell, Associated Supermarket, Perfect French Cleaners, University Drugs, Klein's Butcher Shop, and Jose's Bodega.

While I loved getting out of the projects, I was scared all the time in my new neighborhood. Though the buildings were beautiful, iconic even, my new neighborhood was more dangerous. The kids were in gangs and the gangs were divided along racial lines. The streets were tense.

The tension was escalating at home, too. Why? My dad was getting drunker and meaner. My mom was harried and sad and rapidly falling into more and more depression and denial. I was losing my sister Amy to adolescence as she dealt with her own trauma and turmoil. As far as my brother, Richard, he was lost in his own world, often victimized by the outer world. He was my charge and, for the most part, I stepped up to the plate and took care of him. My mother tried to parent Richard but she had all she could handle dealing with a violent alcoholic husband and holding down nursing jobs at emergency rooms in the South Bronx.

Rabbi Cohen wasn't the only person who had an inkling that I had a tough home life; Isaac's mother saw it as well. After a few visits to Isaac's house, Ma made clear to me, through her grace, hospitality, and warmth, that I was welcome in their home, anytime, day or night. She understood. Through that spring of my sixth grade and the summer, if I wasn't at Rabbi Cohen's apartment, you could find me at Isaac's place.

As a rule, me and Amy never brought friends to our apartment. We were ashamed to. Isaac was the first friend that I brought home to meet my family. He only came over a few times, but right away, Amy fell in love with him. Then again, she was fifteen and, from what I remember, she was falling in love with everybody: Black guys, Puerto Rican guys, white guys. But, only for a day or two.

My mom was happy I had an older male friend in my life and even Richard took a liking to Isaac knowing Isaac would look out for him on the street. From time to time my old man put Isaac to work as a helper alongside me in my dad's remodeling business. I loved how my family was so open and accepting of my new friend. But even so we spent most of our time on his block, with his family, at his apartment, especially when my old man was drinking, which was most of the time.

Every Sunday, me and Isaac practiced our basketball plays at 104. Other days, we played stickball, stoopball, and Skully on Nelson Avenue in front of his building. We didn't go to the same school. Boy, I wish we had. I sorely needed my big brother at 82 with me.

One winter day, I got what turned out to be the worst of the beatdowns as I was coming back to school after lunch. I lived about three blocks from 82, so quite often I went home for lunch. On this particular day, I wish I hadn't. A frigid day with snow squalls and intermediate blinding whiteouts. I could hardly see two feet in front of me. I came up the block and approached the back of the school where I had to enter into the lower schoolyard through a hole in the fence. Then I had to make my way over to the stairs, up to the courtyard, and into the back entrance of the school building before the bell rang for homeroom. The schoolyard was at least two hundred feet across. In between the whiteouts and the gusts of wind, I was traveling about ten feet a minute. I knew I was going to be late and in trouble. Again.

I was already in trouble due to lateness, minor fights, and my disrespectful attitude towards Mr. Goldstein, my math teacher, who was constantly on my case. He had to have been maybe 5-foot-2 and all of 120 pounds. At twelve, I was already 5-foot-7 and a 155 pounds. It wasn't only his diminutive stature as much as it was how he always bragged about himself being a military man. He would order me to give him twenty, meaning pushups, because I snickered when he talked about his fantastical escapades in the National Guard.

William Murphy, my partner in crime in the back of the room, would always egg me on, and I'd be the one to get in trouble. The thing is, we both liked math and were good at it. We just found Mr. Goldstein intolerable at times. So, on this one day I gave him his twenty, and then for good measure, five more with one arm. I wasn't only trying to irritate Mr. Goldstein, I was also showing off in front of a couple of girls, namely Rachel Skorsky and Fern Isaac. Especially Fern or Ferny as she liked to be called. She was the only Black kid in the whole enrichment program and we had a bit of chemistry, mostly of the teasing variety. She would tease me and I would pretend to ignore her. She would laugh, and then laugh some more and I would try to stifle my laughter. That's all I remember about junior high school chemistry. I may be wrong but I think biology was on her mind. I'm not sure. Girls are still hard to figure out.

After my fifth one-armed push-up, I sprung up, saluted Mr. Goldstein and said, "Mr. Army Man, top that!"

In front of the whole class, Mr. Goldstein, red faced and puffing, snorted, "Bernstein, you are insubordinate and your parent needs to come in and have a conference with me." I didn't even know what insubordinate meant. The parent I told this to was my father. The crazy alcoholic but also the World War II bomber pilot war hero. My dad couldn't wait to go see Mr. Goldstein and discuss his insubordinate son. And I'm sure other select topics as well.

Back to the schoolyard. I was trying to get through the blizzard to the other side of the schoolyard, when off to my left, coming through the side gate was a darkish mass moving towards me. I had already heard the late bell ring so, by rights, no one should have been in the schoolyard. I was approaching the flight of stairs to the upper courtyard and could now see that the darkish moving mass was four kids. It seemed strange that anybody would be out in this weather, and coming at me rather than heading into the school building. The gang of four continued moving towards me. It was obvious that our two trajectories were headed towards a mid-schoolyard collision, shy of the staircase I needed to get to. I couldn't avoid this inevitable collision. The blinding whiteout, the head wind, and the now foot and a half of snow I was trudging through made running away impossible.

Even if I could run, there were four of them. And I knew them all: Clifford, Clayton, and Calvin were brothers and their cousin Rodney Rochester, a muscular and menacing midget. Me and Isaac had beaten all of them on the court. They didn't like being victims of the hustle, nor seeing me goof around with Fern. A few weeks earlier, Clayton and Calvin had cornered me in the stairwell, hit me hard in the stomach, and gave me a few final kicks on their way up the stairs to class. I believe Isaac had had some words with them after that attack, but I guess to no avail.

Here I was in the schoolyard, surrounded by the four of them in a swirling blizzard of whiteness. Freezing cold. Wind. But the one good thing was the foot and a half of snow underfoot. Ballast.

Just that past Sunday, my dad had happened to give me some timely advice. I was working down on West Fourth Street in the Village with my old man and his crew remodeling an off-Broadway theater. Me and my dad were in a trench in front of the theater running a main drain line under the sidewalk. We noticed three guys across the street stalking a woman a few feet in front of them, making lewd comments as she walked down the street alone. Because of her wobbly and erratic gate, I guessed she had had a drink or two.

My dad quickly pushed himself up and out of the trench and said, "Steve, wait here. Watch the tools and make sure no one falls into the trench. I'll be right back."

"Wait. Dad, what are you doing? Let me go with you."

As he stepped off the curb to cross the street, he turned back and yelled, "Listen to me. I told you to stay here. Watch the tools. Don't let anybody fall into the trench. I'll be right back." He crossed the street and started following the guys who were following the woman. I could see that he was about forty feet behind them but then I lost sight of everyone when they turned into an alley about two hundred feet further down the block. I sat on the sidewalk, my feet dangling down into the trench, ready with a hammer in my hand.

Less than ten minutes later, my dad emerged from the alley and turned back onto West Fourth Street. His right hand was clenched into a fist, raw and cut up. Other than that bloody fist, he was calm and nothing else was amiss. He sat down opposite me on the sidewalk, his feet dangling down into the trench like mine. I asked, "Is the lady okay? Did they do anything to her?"

He didn't answer. All he said was, "Put the hammer down. I wanna tell you something. I wanna tell you how

STORIES FROM THE STOOP

to handle yourself if you gotta fight more than one." As he talked, I glanced down at his bloodied fist, clenching and unclenching. And then he told me, "You take your right fist and you squeeze it as hard as you can, all while you are focusing on one—not all of 'em, just one. You set your sights and you clench your fist. The best hope you got is you put down one. They see it and then they all run away. If there is a gang after you, they are, by definition, cowards so you hurt the one." I took this all in and realized, maybe I had been lucky that I hadn't needed this advice up until that point in my life.

In that schoolyard, in that blizzard, those guys wanted me dead. Mainly because I was a white kid in their neighborhood, hanging around with their people.

In that instant, my dad's words came back to me from four days earlier. Call it prophetic, call it luck: *When they come for you, you take down one. Just the one.*

The older one, Clayton, yelled, "Get 'im!" He made the first move, both arms raised, going for my head and neck. The three others were behind Clayton, moving in fast to tackle me. I stepped back with my right foot and firmly planted it into the deep snow. I pivoted my body to my right and cocked my right elbow straight back and then, with everything I had, I torqued my upper body forward, leading with my fist clenched hard, solid like a brick. I aimed right for his nose. I heard a snap. Clayton went down. The snow went crimson. The other guys stopped inches and seconds short of nailing me, their eyes bulging in shock. Clayton was on the ground, in the snow, bleeding and swearing. The guys scooped Clayton up, blood pouring out of his broken nose. They scurried off, leaving a thin dark trail of blood back to the gate they came in from.

My dad had been right. It worked. I got the one and scared the rest. My heart was racing. All that blood truly scared me. And beyond that one moment, I had a premonition: this was only the beginning. Worse was coming my way. Revenge.

Other than my bloodied right fist, not a scratch on me. I continued on my snowy trek up the stairs to the upper schoolyard, to the big metal double doors of the school building. I was ten minutes late and the doors were locked. With my good fist, I banged on the door until a monitor opened it. I climbed the three flights of stairs to my homeroom. With my eyes downcast, I entered the classroom and made my way to my seat. Mr. Gordon, my homeroom and social studies teacher, stared at me. As did all the kids. No one said a word.

Mr. Gordon came over and asked me if everything was okay. He always made me feel respected and appreciated. I liked him. I was definitely shook up and he saw right away that something must have happened. I was too afraid to say anything and hadn't yet figured out how to explain what had happened.

Within two minutes of me sitting down, Mr. Feinberg, the assistant principal, pushed the door open, bolted into the room, and while still holding onto the doorknob, leaned in, pointed to me and blurted out, "Bernstein, I need to see you right away. In my office. Now." *Oh shit! Did I kill Clayton? I'm dead.*

I stood up as Mr. Feinberg held the door for me and we walked the few steps across the hall to his office. Already waiting for me inside the office were Mrs. Shipmann, the principal, Mr. Glick, my gym teacher, and a cop. Mr. Feinberg and Mr. Gordon followed me into the office and closed the door. Mr. Feinberg said, "Sit down. Your mother is on her way." I wish they had called my father instead. He would have understood.

They told me Clayton got terribly hurt and was in the emergency room. His mother was on her way to the school to press charges.

On each of their faces was a look of concern and confusion. "So, Steve, what happened?" Mrs. Shipmann asked. I took in everybody's worried faces and breathed in deeply. I was still wound up over the whole thing.

The people in the room knew me. They knew I had had some relatively minor behavioral issues. They had met my dad because he was the parent usually called in. Just like Rabbi Cohen and Ma, they all sensed that life was tough for me at home. Because of their suspicions, these administrators and teachers had often looked out for me.

I told them what had happened. As soon as I finished the story, Mr. Feinberg left his office to round up the three other guys and bring them into the adjacent office. He asked the cop to go speak with them. As Calvin, Clifford, and Clayton passed by Mr. Feinberg's office, I saw them leer at me through the glass window in the wooden door. I was petrified.

Mrs. Shipmann asked, "So, let me get this straight, there was one of you and four of them, right? So, they came after you and then you hit Clayton. Very, very hard."

"Yeah. I was scared." I told them what my father had taught me. I saw understanding and empathy in their eyes.

All of a sudden, Clayton's mom burst into Mr. Feinberg's office. She was screaming and crying. She pointed at me, demanding that I be punished. When they were able to settle her down, Mrs. Shipmann repeated what I had just told her. After Clayton's mom heard the story, she stood up and calmly walked out into the hallway to the adjacent office where the cop and the three other guys were waiting. I heard muffled words, loud voices, and the door slam. After a minute or two, I saw her pass by the door of Mr. Feinberg's office and storm down the hall. She was fuming.

The cop came in and, with a curious smile, said, "As crazy as it sounds, Steve's story pans out." From that moment on, I was branded. All at once, I was about to become revered and reviled.

Mr. Feinberg said, "Steve, I got my eye on you, take care of yourself."

Mr. Gordon put his hand on my shoulder and walked me back to his classroom. Nobody was there. Everybody was off to their classes. We sat down and talked until the bell rang. Mr. Gordon said, "You have two more years here, Steve. It's not going to be easy. Let me know if there is anything I can do to help."

After school, when Isaac got wind of what had happened, he tracked me down and made me tell him everything. He smiled, gave me a big hug and asked, "Isn't thirteen about becoming a man?"

"Yeah," I said.

"Welcome to the club." And then with a worried look, he added, "It ain't gonna be easy. I'll help you the best I can." With that I felt better.

So, with Isaac's protective vigilance on the street after school, my life wasn't as bad as I had feared. I was down to about two fights per week at school. I was doing better in my classes and acted up less in Mr. Goldstein's class. He found some new respect for me, not just because of the incident in the snow or my improved behavior, but also because my dad had gone in to see him. I guess my old man had straightened him out.

As my bar mitzvah was approaching, I practiced my Torah recitation in the basement of our building much of that summer. It was cold, damp, and dark, but the acoustics were great. Plus, in the basement I could get out of the apartment and be alone and focus.

A few times Isaac came over and listened to me practice. He had never heard Hebrew before, but liked the language and the melody. He would sit on the wooden basement steps and listen. One time after my practice, he complimented me: "It ain't Motown, but you sound damn good!" It's a good thing Isaac didn't ask me what the Hebrew words meant. Not a clue. Understanding the words wasn't part of the deal.

The day of my bar mitzvah arrived, a late September Saturday. I got up early that morning to meet the rabbi for one last run-through. He wanted my recitation to be perfect. He was proud of me. Because I had never actually set foot inside the synagogue itself, Rabbi Cohen had me practice on the dais in front of the empty pews, the real deal, so I would be more comfortable. He reviewed his notes and set up the large gilded Torah to the spot where I would read from. I looked out at the immense sanctuary hall, large enough to accommodate three hundred people. I watched as the pews started filling up. It surprised me to find out that there were still enough Jews in the neighborhood to fill up the synagogue.

Isaac, unfazed by his first visit to a synagogue, strolled in like he owned the joint, followed first by my Black friends and then Jose Gonzales, who brought up the rear of the entourage. At the entrance, older Jewish men greeted each of my guys with a "Shabbat Shalom," a handshake, a prayer shawl, and a yarmulke. Plus, a few raised eyebrows. My guys knew what to do with the handshake. For the rest, well the men at the door had to help them out.

My friends and family filled up the front rows of the synagogue. Rabbi Cohen stood on the dais and began the service by scanning the congregation, smiling and nodding his greetings as people settled in. When his eyes came to the front center row, he beamed his biggest smile and remarked, "Never have I seen such a colorful bar mitzvah ceremony."

I could see what he meant. That center front row had all my friends in it: four Black kids, and a Puerto Rican kid, flanked by Richard on one end and my cousin Mitchel on the other end. All dressed up, with yarmulkes on their heads and prayer shawls around their shoulders. What a day!

Me and Jose had been in the fifth grade together at 104. That was the year he told me how he was indebted to me forever. I had helped him conceal the fact that he had peed in his pants at school. That afternoon I had helped him get home unmolested. "Friends for life!" he had proclaimed.

Me and Mitchel were more like brothers than cousins. We saw each other a lot because my dad and my dad's older brother, Irving, Mitchel's father, drank together. Mitchel called on me to beat up kids who were picking on him in his neighborhood.

Rabbi Cohen stood next to me on the dais. He used a *yad*, a silver Torah pointer, to guide me, line by line through the ornate parchment pages. I was totally at ease. I thoroughly enjoyed myself and appreciated hearing my voice and the melody that I had worked so hard on. It was almost as if the sounds were coming from somewhere else and I was just listening. That's how easy it was. Having worked so hard with the rabbi for months, having him by my side encouraging me now, seeing the proud and happy faces of my friends and family, as well as the admiration of the rest of the congregation who I had never even met, was a peaceful and joyous moment, the likes of which I had never experienced before.

I breezed through my reading. When I finished, Rabbi Cohen leaned over and whispered, "Bernstein, fabulous." Everyone stood up and clapped. The rabbi, a big smile on his face, took me by the elbow to introduce me to the congregants. All of them, and it was a full house that day. Everyone complemented me on how well I had read and how confident and mature I was. At least that's what I think they said; they mostly spoke Yiddish to the rabbi. Susan, the rabbi's daughter, came over and gave me a big hug.

After Rabbi Cohen was finished showing me off—and not to forget I was the kid who got kicked out of his Hebrew school—my friends and family who had been waiting patiently came over to congratulate me. Amy hugged me, tears of joy streaming down her face. My dad had a big smile on his face and for the first time ever, we shook hands. Like men. He said, "Congratulations, son," and then walked straight over to Rabbi Cohen, patted him on the back, and shook his hand vigorously. Included in the handshake was a wad of cash. Rabbi Cohen smiled graciously and smoothly slipped the bills into the pocket of his suit jacket. I couldn't hear exactly what they were saying, but I knew they were speaking Yiddish and they were smiling and laughing. The rabbi had prepared me well for that day, prepared me well for the rest of my life. That day, I became a man.

Isaac and the rest of the crew were all polished and dressed up but it was clear from their stiffness that they couldn't wait to get out of their suits and ties and Jewish gear. After they patted me on the back, their attention was mostly focused on food, especially the honey sponge cake they kept eyeballing.

I was relieved that Uncle Irving and my dad weren't drunk that day in the synagogue—they saved their drinking for the reception. Halfway through the party at the rented hall, Uncle Irving brought out a large A & P supermarket shopping bag and proceeded to load up with cold cuts, chopped liver, potato knishes, rye bread, challah bread, half-empty bottles of Manischewitz, and, worst of all, the uneaten half of my blue and white frosted bar mitzvah cake. I never did get a piece.

Four years later, after I graduated high school, I went back to check out the old neighborhood. The Jewish deli, Ronais Delicatessen, that had catered my reception, was now a bodega. The synagogue itself had closed down and was now a methadone clinic.

The week following my bar mitzvah, me and Isaac both went up to the world-famous Eddy's Bike Shop on Jerome Avenue and 181st Street where we bought ourselves two brand new Schwinn ten-speed Continental bicycles, top of the line, chrome forks and all. Me with my money from my part-time jobs and my bar mitzvah, and Isaac with money, mostly from his new betting business he had recently started with his uncle.

We got to know The Bronx from a whole new perspective atop shiny new bikes, rolling like royalty through the streets. My Continental was midnight blue and Isaac's British green. Both bikes were decked out with fox tails streaming from the handlebars and baseball cards attached to the spokes with clothespins for sound effects. Life was looking up.

A few days after we got our new bikes, Isaac paid me a visit at Klein's Kosher Butcher Shop on Featherbed Lane where I worked after school making deliveries and cleaning up at the end of the day. My job had originally been Isaac's but he had moved up in the world to delivering groceries by bicycle for the A & P supermarket so he brought me in to take his place at Klein's. He trained me to deliver meat to the older Jewish people still left in the neighborhood as they couldn't, or wouldn't, go out on the street themselves anymore. I usually netted a quarter from each delivery. Some of the cheapskates gave me their return soda and seltzer bottles instead of coins, two cents a bottle. The owners, Mr. and Mrs. Klein, loved Isaac. He lived right around the corner, he was polite, diligent, and an all-around great employee. Because I was three years younger than him, the Kleins had their concerns when

Isaac introduced me. But, with his mentoring, in no time I was almost as good as him.

It was now October 1967, a year since me and Isaac had met. By that point the basketball business was over and all we had for money was what we earned at our afterschool jobs, plus Isaac's betting business. His uncle, or whatever one of those guys was in his apartment, was a bookie and would take bets on ballgames and horses. Isaac was his apprentice because his uncle couldn't read. One of Isaac's main job requirements was to read the paper every day. Isaac would get a handle on the box scores, races, and games coming up and all the other pertinent information necessary to conduct a lucrative betting operation. Also, as apprentice, Isaac collected bets and did payouts all over the neighborhood. Our early training in the basketball hustling business prepared him well for this promotion, as it were.

When I showed up to work at Klein's after school one afternoon, Isaac was sitting on a milk crate outside on the sidewalk in front of the butcher shop. He had the *Daily News* in his hands, but rather than reading the sports page for his job as usual, he was intently looking at the front page. He glanced up and said, "Hey Steve, isn't this your dad on the front page of the paper?"

Sure enough, there was my dad in black and white. He was being escorted out of the Bronx County Courthouse on 161st Street on either side by two men in suits. My dad had a newspaper in his hand and was attempting to cover up his face, but right there it said Hyman Bernstein was convicted of extortion and found guilty by Mayor Lindsay's task force on city corruption.

Come to find out, during his seventeen years as a city building inspector, my old man ran a crew of other building inspectors who moonlighted on city time and took bribes from landlords who paid him *not* to condemn their buildings. They also were coerced into hiring him to renovate them. If the landlords didn't cooperate they could be certain that their building would have a very hard time getting approved by the building department. So, my old man collected his city pay, took the bribes, got the contract to fix the buildings, and then paid his crew. His crew were the other building inspectors. They all paid buddies in the office to punch in for them, when necessary. And, the office buddies got paid, too. My old man was the ringleader of these other guys who, like himself, were tradesmen as well as building inspectors. Pressure from Mayor Lindsay's task force resulted in every member of my dad's crew choosing to rat him out, rather than spend time in jail and lose their jobs and pensions. My old man lost his job three years away from a full pension. I don't remember him doing jail time but Isaac was impressed anyway. He saw my dad in a whole new light.

Not Mrs. Miller though. She was the landlady of the apartment we lived in. She had been looking for a way to kick us out anyway. She hated the company that me and Amy kept. Too dark for her liking. She hated my father coming in loud and drunk. So this was it. She finally had a good reason not to renew our lease: "no criminals in her apartment building."

A month later, in November, our lease was up and we were out. This time we moved about ten blocks further south and east in The Bronx, which by all measures, was a step backwards. The Bronx, especially our new neighborhood in the South Bronx, was ablaze in a wildfire of crime that took everything and everybody in its wake. We moved to this fabulous art deco type building, built in the thirties, east of the Grand Concourse near 167th Street that was just beautiful. Parquet floors, sunken living room, and not one, but two bathrooms! Unheard of. The apartments were to die for. Too bad you couldn't go out in the street, or else you very well could die.

I had a new neighborhood but I chose to finish up the remaining months of the school year at 82. Me and Isaac didn't see each other anywhere near as much as before but I made new friends. One reason was the school days were much longer for me. In the old neighborhood I walked three blocks to school. Now, to get to and from 82, I had to take the number 2 bus on the Concourse and then the Tremont Avenue bus. All told, about an hour each way every day, for the rest of the year until I graduated from junior high school.

That summer of 1968, me and Isaac got to hang out more. I spent many nights at his house, just like the old days. We would ride our bikes and play ball on Nelson

Avenue, just the two of us. The best time we had that summer was when the temperature would hit the nineties and we would take the bus over the Washington Bridge and then walk south on Amsterdam Avenue to the Highbridge public pool where, for ten cents, you got to cool off in clean, heavily chlorinated water in gigantic pools with literally thousands of other kids. If it wasn't for Isaac being with me, I would have died several times over, being the only white kid in the pool.

The only other option to cool off was opening the fire hydrant on my block. We would dart in and out of the solid jet of water, standing three or four feet away from the hydrant, any closer and you would get knocked over from the high pressure. To open up the hydrant, I borrowed the two-foot-long Stillson monkey wrench from my dad's plumbing van. It was steel and weighed about twelve pounds. That bought me some respect in my new neighborhood. All summer long on the hottest days, the little kids would track me down in the school yard and beg, "Can you turn the water on. Pleeeeease."

In September 1968, I turned fourteen and started tenth grade at DeWitt Clinton High School. Life got real busy. I still had a long commute in the morning on the number two bus. In the afternoon, I had to take the number 4 train all the way down to Lexington and 54th. From two to five every afternoon after school, I delivered packages, parcels, and letters all over midtown for Acme Messenger Service.

When us messenger boys, mostly teenagers, arrived for our shift, we would check in with Abe, the boss, who stood behind a long Formica counter. Abe was short and round. He had salt and pepper hair like Brillo, black-rimmed glasses, and was always chewing on a lit cigar, stinking up the place. We sat in folding chairs along the wall until Abe yelled out, "Bernstein. Next. Hurry up. Let's go." Abe gave us tokens for the subway and buses and a specific deadline by which time we had to be back with the parcels we picked up along the way. Instead of using the tokens, I ran to each delivery in order to make good time. Plus, I liked the exercise. Ten or so tokens a day meant a pocketful of tokens by Friday.

The pace of the afternoons alternated between racing through the streets of midtown Manhattan and then back again to Acme Messenger Service, waiting on a folding chair.

One afternoon as I was waiting for Abe to call my name, I was surprised to see a man in a bow tie and a plaid sports coat sit down in the folding chair next to me. He took off his fedora and leaned his cane on the wall between our two chairs. When he introduced himself to me, I recognized his accent. Yiddish. Mr. Cantor was a seventy-five-year-old messenger boy. His wife had died of cancer and he was living on Social Security. To make ends meet, he had to do this job. He wasn't complaining.

Every Friday before sundown, Mr. Cantor headed home early to observe the Sabbath. One Friday afternoon

I went to find him before he left so I could give him the tokens I had saved up all week. The first time I offered Mr. Cantor my tokens, he was surprised but also grateful. That became our Friday ritual.

The year 1968 was pivotal for me. A job downtown. My friendship with Mr. Cantor. A new tougher neighborhood. Still the wrong color, though. Joined a gang. Started high school. Wolf. My first real girlfriend (tell you about that in the next story). The music was sublime, but the times were turbulent for me. And for the country.

Me and Isaac didn't see each other as much because of our jobs, living in two different neighborhoods and going to two different schools. So we decided, for old time's sake, to resurrect the basketball hustle by bringing it to a new venue. There was one court left that we hadn't gone to during our hustling days. It was a full court in a large park located inside the projects where I used to live. The park wasn't one of those green parks; it was asphalt, cement, and chain-link fences. No grass. No trees. In addition to the basketball court, there were squash courts, though they were only used for handball, along with monkey bars, swings, and giant cement animals for the little kids to climb on.

After an early dinner at Isaac's, we walked over to the basketball court up at the projects. It was a warm early spring evening, April 4, 1968, still light out and the park was jumping.

STORIES FROM THE STOOP

Just like in the old days, Isaac always knew a couple of the guys and started talking us up. They looked over at me, the little white kid, snickered, then back at Isaac, talked amongst themselves, and finally came back with some cash to lay the bet. Granted, me and Isaac had been playing basketball on our own together from time to time, but it had been many months since we actually had done the hustle. After no less than two minutes into the game, we were back. Same as before, maybe better. Our plays were flowing to perfection. We were up by three, then five, and then it got to be 10–4 ours, point game.

The sounds of Motown filled the air. A transistor radio coat-hangered to the chain-link fence was blaring Marvin Gaye, the Supremes, and the Temptations. As I was about to take the ball out at the foul line to finish these guys off, the music stopped. After a second or two the announcer came on and said, "The Reverend Martin Luther King was shot and killed today in Memphis by a white man." The basketballs stopped bouncing. The park turned eerily silent. It seemed like even the busses and cars out on University Avenue and on the Cross Bronx Expressway stopped. All the ballplayers stood still, intently listening to that radio hung on the chain-link fence.

All this in an instant, me with the basketball in my hand at the foul line, ready to take it out for the win. The announcement didn't hit me as quick as it did everybody else.

All around the country, not only in The Bronx, riots, marches, violent and nonviolent confrontations, and demonstrations were making the headlines. Through my friendship with Isaac, I had learned about the civil rights movement and, in particular, the message of Dr. King. In contrast to all the violence I read about and witnessed myself, I learned from Isaac that Dr. King stood for nonviolence.

As usual, I was the only white kid in the park. I looked around the court and saw the faces of the other ball players go from shock, comprehension, sadness, and finally, to rage. In a flash, Isaac processed it all and then got busy. He took the ball from me, coolly placed it on the foul line, and without revealing any panic, he firmly grabbed my arm, and side-by-side he calmly walked me out the park gate, down the walkway to University Avenue. As we left the court, we heard a chant rising, "Whitey killed the king, whitey killed the king."

We started to sprint once we hit Featherbed Lane. Isaac was ahead of me, and kept looking back at me, yelling, "Steve, keep up!" It all happened so quickly, I was still in a daze but I started to get the sense that we, or maybe I, was running for my life. I caught glimpses of Isaac's face. When he looked back at me I saw tears running down his cheeks.

In less than five minutes, we got to Isaac's apartment. We barged in and collapsed on the living room floor. Everybody was home. Ma, all the kids, and the dads were crowded around the staticky black and white TV. They were crying. On the TV, Walter Cronkite, just about in tears himself, was relating to the whole world what happened to Dr. Martin Luther King.

Everyone stared at us, startled, eyes unfocused. When they realized it was us, they jumped up off the sofas and chairs and got up off the floor and all together reached out to us, in one big family embrace. It lasted a long time. Finally, Isaac said, "Ma, we're gonna keep Steve here for a while, until things die down and it's safe on the street, safe enough for him to go home." One of the dads slowly backed out of the circle and walked over to the apartment door behind me. I heard him lock the door. Click. Click.

Early the next morning, I made my way home and laid low for several days as per Isaac's instructions. He told me not to come by; he would come looking for me at my place. We talked on the phone a few times and after three weeks, we picked up again. He and I weren't that much different, but the world around us was changed forever. I was confused. I was so far removed from the mentality of that white man who had pulled the trigger, but I couldn't get that chant, "Whitey killed the king, whitey killed the king," out of my head for a long, long, time.

It was getting harder and harder for me and Isaac to get together. The world had evolved as did our own lives. After seven months in my new neighborhood, I had begun to make new friends. A loosely formed gang on my block gave me an honorary membership. In spite of me being the wrong color, allowances were made.

Isaac told me his whole family was preparing to move back to Delaware in a few weeks. Some bad shit had happened on Nelson Avenue. His sister Yvette was attacked right on their stoop and after that, he told me Ma had said, "Enough! That's it! I'm goin' back home to Delaware."

The first time Isaac came to my new neighborhood was also the last time. Me and my new friends—Octavio, Dee, Skip, Peggy, Allie, and Roberto—were all sitting on my stoop when Isaac rode over on his Schwinn Continental. From the outside it seemed like we were all shooting the shit on the stoop and playing stoop ball and Skully, but really the guys were all preoccupied with Peggy and her generous breasts.

Isaac got off his bike, put the kickstand down, and came over to me and shook my hand and ruffled my hair. He was happy to see me but was not impressed with my new friends. Isaac laughed at the way Roberto played stoopball. Roberto kept missing the pointy edge of the step on the stoop with his Pensy Pinkie ball. He fancied himself a baseball superstar and was embarrassed. I had found out that his name wasn't Roberto. I heard his mother calling for him out the window one day. She was yelling, "Albert, Albert, comida!" So, I asked him why he called himself Roberto, when his mom called him Albert. He said his hero was Roberto Clemente, the great Puerto

Rican baseball player, and so he decided to change his name.

Stoopball was a mini version of baseball with singles, doubles, triples, and home runs. It could be played with as few as one player on each team. The batter stood on the sidewalk and had to throw down the ball on the point of the stoop step and try to get as long a hit as possible. Hitting the building across the street was a home run. Various points along the way, a car fender, a manhole or a fire hydrant, were lesser hits. Hits were also determined by the number of bounces before the ball was caught. If the ball was caught on the fly by the other team, that was an out.

Isaac also snickered at the lame Skully caps we were using. I felt the same about them, but I never said anything. That's why I wasn't playing that afternoon; Skully was never the same without Isaac.

Skully was a citywide game. Every neighborhood played it differently. It was an on-the-street game of skill and luck. Literally, on the street. With either thick chalk or spray paint, we would draw a ten-foot by ten-foot square. In the center was a square for number 13 and all along the perimeter were squares for numbers 1 through 12 located in such a way so that you had to crisscross the board to get from one number to the next.

If you were a Skully player, you always had your favorite Skully caps with you in your pocket. They were usually a soda bottle cap, filled with melted Crayola crayons to give them weight and ballast. Melties we called them. To play, you get on your hands and knees at the starting line, and you flick your Skully cap with your middle finger and thumb, attempting to get the cap into square number one, not touching any lines. From there you flick your cap to square number 2, and so on until you get to square number 13 in the center. And, if you can, back again. The reason why some players preferred melties was the melted crayon gave the cap extra mass so you could bump other caps out of the game. If you bumped one cap three times in a row, you killed that player.

Isaac was a master at the game. Back on Nelson Avenue, I saw him go around the Skully board, non-stop, square to square, all the way to the number 13 square in the middle. And then back again to square one. No one else even took their Skully caps out of their pockets. Why bother?

With the cockiness of a Skully master, Isaac waltzed over to the Skully board on the street in front of my stoop where Dee and Octavio were playing. Isaac picked up one of their Skully caps, turned it over in his hand, brought it up to eye level, flipped it over again, held it in the palm of his hand to assess its weight, and then, finally, laughed. "What the fuck is this? Are you kidding me?" he asked, and then slowly let the meltie roll out of his hand, and drop back onto the Skully board.

Isaac thought little of my new friends and their Skully caps. Back in our heyday on Nelson Avenue, we didn't use bottle caps. Not us. Me and Isaac used the round ornaments that sat either on the fenders or hoods of the cars from the fifties and sixties. They were the perfect round shape, mass, and size for Skully. We were well known for our Skully caps; I had a T-bird and he had a Caddy. You got to understand, you couldn't buy or make these things; you had to go out and break them off the cars when no one was around and pray to God the car owner never caught up with you. Sometimes they did. Not pretty.

After Isaac finished insulting everyone, my friends cleared out. Me and Isaac had the stoop to ourselves. So, I said to Isaac, "Delaware, huh? Where the fuck is Delaware?" He said, "South." He said it kind of sadly. He wrote down his new address and said, "You better come down for a visit. And, by the way, watch your back. I don't trust your friends." His attitude towards my friends turned out to be well founded. A few weeks later, in mid-May, Isaac moved south.

My street friends went to Taft High School up on 170th Street, about three blocks away. Or they didn't go to school at all. Instead of Taft, I chose DeWitt Clinton High School, one of the best public high schools in all five boroughs. It was an all-boys high school with about eight thousand students divided into three shifts, starting at different times during the day. It was way up on the Grand Concourse in the North Bronx, near Mosholu Parkway, which is why I had to take the number 2 bus forty minutes each way. In addition to academics, DeWitt Clinton was also renowned for its athletics, so it offered me the chance to focus on both, which I loved. I didn't get into one fight at DeWitt Clinton. Rather, I thrived there. But back on my block, life was hell and Isaac wasn't around to help.

Over the next two years me and Isaac exchanged a few letters. We wrote on white loose leaf lined paper, folded many times to fit into the envelope. He wrote in print and I wrote in cursive. I told him all about the adventures I was having and how right he had been about my so-called buddies. He wrote about being a center on his high school basketball team. He said life was different, but everyone was doing okay. Isaac said he was doing okay too, but I was never quite convinced. He told me that in two years he hadn't been able to get a job. The Isaac I knew always had a job. Or two. Or three. He was feeling pessimistic about his chances of going to college.

It wasn't until June 1970 that I found my way clear to follow Isaac's orders to visit him in Delaware, two years after he had moved. That May I had started making plans. Even though I no longer had Mr. Gordon, my social studies teacher from junior high, we had kept in touch. I thought he would be my best resource to help me figure out how to get to Delaware. One afternoon when I had only a half day of school, I visited Mr. Gordon over his lunch break. We took down some of the maps he had up on the wall and he showed me where Delaware was in relation to The Bronx. Wilmington, where Isaac told me to take the train to, was more than two hundred miles away. Mr. Gordon asked, "Are you sure you don't want someone to drive you? It's a long, long ways away. Are you sure your father can't take you?"

"No way."

"Nobody else?" he asked.

"Nope. I'm takin' the train."

Mr. Gordon told me if he had had a car, he would have driven me. It was obvious he didn't think it was a good idea for me to go alone all that way. Nonetheless he helped me make a plan. After the maps of the states, he pulled out some subway maps and a Penn Central passenger rail schedule. He knew about trains because he told me he was originally from Philadelphia and took them all the time to visit his family back home. He showed me that I could take the subway down to the nearly completed reconstruction of Penn Station and get on the Penn Central all the way to Wilmington. The whole thing was going to set me back about twenty-eight bucks. Round trip. Pocket change for me with all my part-time jobs.

The other thing Mr. Gordon told me was that life was different down in Delaware. He showed me the Mason-Dixon Line and how Delaware was a slave state back before the Civil War, meaning that attitudes about race were very different there. I kind of understood, but with the assassination of Dr. King, riots, and integration, I couldn't help but hope that race relations had to be getting better, even down south. But more to the point, I couldn't believe Isaac would move to a place where Black people were worse off than they were in The Bronx.

When I told my parents I was going to Delaware to visit Isaac, they didn't seem too nervous that I was going all by myself on this big trip. I had the money saved and for the first time in the three and a half years that I had known Isaac, our moms talked, just to make sure everybody was on the same page.

When I told my friends I was going to Delaware by train to see Isaac, they thought I was nuts. Most of us growing up in The Bronx seldom left the neighborhoods. Maybe we would take the subway downtown for something, like for my messenger job for example, but hardly ever out of the city, let alone out of state.

I was going to be away for a total of four days. I felt like a big shot. It was the first time I packed my own suitcase. I included a couple days' worth of fresh clothes, one set of good clothes, and my dress pair of sneakers, sparkling white high top Pro Keds. For the trip itself, I wore my not-so-white everyday Converse high tops. I had my Pros and Cons with me. I was ready for anything. I had a lot of cash, way more than I needed, about thirty bucks in singles and fives, the twenty-eight dollars for the ticket, plus a pocket full of change for phone calls and incidentals. My mother packed me a tuna fish sandwich on Wonder bread and an apple for the road.

STORIES FROM THE STOOP

On my way to catch the subway to get to Penn Station, I realized I was looking forward to seeing Isaac and his family, but also to being in the country as Isaac had described it in his letters: grass, trees, private houses, yards. I imagined clean streets and fresh air. I was glad to get away from the slummy Bronx buildings and the noise, congestion, smog, dog shit, trash, crime, and fear, even if it was just for a few days.

Isaac had told me they were living in a private house, owned by his mother and her two sisters, all three families together under one roof. I imagined the houses would be white painted wood with a picket fence around a big green lawn. Up until this trip, my only other experience in a private house, as opposed to a brick tenement or project, was my grandfather's tiny cottage upstate, near the Canadian border.

After a whole lot of subway transfers, I finally made it to the Penn Central Line. I got my ticket, found my train, got a window seat and settled in for the four-hour ride. I started to feel kind of expansive, like I was busting out of my shell. I felt mature and worldly. It was the first time I had ever been on a railroad train as opposed to a subway train. This train wasn't crowded, wasn't dirty, wasn't noisy, no one was standing in the aisle, everyone had a seat, it was a smooth ride, it was well lit and airy, it didn't smell, and there was a bathroom. The best part of this ride was not being in a dark subway tunnel. Once the train was out of the city, it was fun seeing the scenery flashing by. But what struck me as most peculiar was that all the passengers were white.

When I got off the train and started to look around, it felt like a different planet. Throughout the station, bright colored spring flowers were overflowing the hanging flower pots. The large windows were spotless and the marble floors and metal countertops were polished and gleaming, so different than the grimy New York subway stations that stunk of piss. You would think that this cleanliness and order would have felt cheerful and welcoming. It didn't. Rather, it felt unnatural and superficial, too clean.

Strangest of all was what I noticed about the people working in the station. All the people behind the counter handling the tickets and money were white. All the janitors, the shoe shine guys, the porters, the guy working at the newspaper stand, and the cab drivers were Black. It reminded me of what Mr. Gordon had said: "Attitudes about race were different down south." It was almost like the ticket counter was a Mason-Dixon Line that ran through the Wilmington station.

I pulled out Isaac's letter with the address and followed Ma's instructions to get a cab from the taxi stand and give the driver the address. In an instant, a porter magically appeared and asked, "Do you need a cab, sir? Can I take your bag, sir? Right this way, sir." At fifteen, no adult man had ever addressed me as sir, and this porter had done it three times in less than thirty seconds. I didn't have to ask for help or figure anything out on my own. It was all done for me. He took my suitcase and I followed him to a waiting taxi. While the porter put my suitcase in the trunk, I wondered what to do about a tip. I had known I would have to tip the cab driver, but having a porter help me had not been part of my plan. I quickly reached into my pocket and grabbed a handful of my phone-and-incidental coins. This was my first incidental. I was so nervous about the whole thing I had no idea how much change I gave him. He held the coins in both hands, and with his eyes facing down towards the sidewalk, he said, "Thank you sir. Oh, thank you sir," as he backed away. I almost expected him to call me master.

The driver was dressed in a black suit with a matching black cap. When I showed him Isaac's address, he gave me a perplexed look and then, quickly, turned back around again and began to drive. Just like the train ride, I enjoyed checking out the scenery and watching the neighborhoods go by, all single family homes on clean streets. Lots of trees. And, every single person we passed was Black.

In twenty minutes we pulled up in front of Isaac's house. It was a large white house with a white fence, more or less like I had imagined. However, instead of a big green lawn, there was a small patch of grass between the house and the sidewalk. The driver got out, walked around the front of the cab, and reached for the door handle, but I had already gotten out using the other door.

I guess I was supposed to wait for him to open my door for me, but I beat him to it. I waited for him to use his key to unlock the trunk so I could get my suitcase. As I reached in, he reached in quicker, gave me a nudge, and swiftly grabbed my bag.

I was getting used to letting people do things for me, even though it didn't feel right. Just like with the porter, this was the cab driver's job. At least this time I was ready with a tip; I had a one-dollar bill in my hand which I gave to him. He said, "Thank you, sir," and put the dollar bill in his jacket pocket, but he didn't give me my suitcase. Instead, he briskly walked past me. I followed him up the walkway towards the side door. I had been so preoccupied with the challenges of the suitcase and the tip, that I hadn't noticed that Isaac's entire family, all fourteen of them, were lined up by the side of the house waiting for me. The cab driver put down my suitcase and I thanked him again. He said, "Thank you, sir," bowed, tipped his hat and, just like the porter, backed away. It had been so awkward all afternoon as I slowly got used to what Mr. Gordon called "the difference," but it was truly embarrassing being treated like a superior in front of Isaac's family, though they didn't seem to notice anything out of the ordinary.

At the head of the line was Isaac, a great big smile on his face. But before he could give me hug, his sisters and brothers got to me first. Lots of hugs and kisses. Next, Ma embraced me warmly. One of the dads shook my hand. Finally, Isaac was able to reach into the pile of peo-ple and gave me a hug that was more like a headlock. He introduced me to Ma's two sisters and all the cousins who didn't know what to make of this happy reunion. They had, of course, heard all about me and knew I was white. However, seeing how much we all loved each other was beyond their comprehension. It was as if they were watching a scene from another planet.

It took about fifteen minutes of meeting and greeting and a meal to where the aunts and the cousins overcame their doubts and worries. Once again I felt like I was with my family. It had been two years since I had seen every-body. All the kids were taller, even Isaac got taller. I sup-pose I had, too. In honor of my arrival, Ma made those grits and collard greens she thought I loved so much and of course I devoured the pigs' feet and pork chops. I think they all got a kick out of how much I loved Ma's cooking.

That night after dinner, Isaac got permission to borrow his aunt's Eldorado to drive me and the three boy cousins, Bernard, Dwayne, and Terry, to Philly to see a drive-in movie. Isaac explained, "When we wanna get away from the bullshit of Delaware, we go north to Philly." I think I was beginning to understand what he was talking about.

Of course during the ride, the subject of basketball came up. Isaac told his cousins how we used to play bas-ketball back in The Bronx. I noticed he left out the part about the hustle. As Dwayne was warming up to me, he suggested that we all play ball the next day. And then he added, "We don't get much of a chance to play basketball together, Blacks and whites. Obviously, the best ball players are Black." To make his point, he rattled off some of his favorites like Hal Greer, Willis Reed, Walt Frazier, Kareem Abdul-Jabbar (then Lew Alcindor), and Oscar Robertson. I didn't disagree. All five of us spent the rest of the ride bantering back and forth about whose team was better—their 76ers or my Knicks.

After about half an hour, as we were pulling into the drive-in, Isaac declared, "Conversation over. The New York Knicks got the best record and they're gonna win the championship." And of course, Isaac was right; the Knicks did win that year.

As usual, Isaac had had the night all planned out for us. But it wasn't until we paid for our tickets that we all found out what movie we were seeing: *Watermelon Man*. The movie was a comedy about a white racist idiot who wakes up one morning with black skin and ends up on the receiving end of racism. We all enjoyed the movie and laughed a lot at this ignorant white guy getting what he deserved. But, I couldn't help but feel self-conscious and ashamed of my whiteness. Isaac and the cousins seemed to be having a great time laughing it up all night. To them I think it was just a funny movie, which it was.

After the movie was over, the conversation naturally turned back to, of course, basketball for the whole ride back to Isaac's house. I never did find out how Isaac and the three cousins felt about the theme of the movie or about having me in the car watching it with them. For me, even though I knew the film was a comedy, it was an important part of my growing understanding of racism and how different the lives of Black people and white people were.

The next day, after the cousins were getting used to having a white kid around, we all started to just be guys. Teens hanging out, talking about girls and basketball and school. Soon enough, I noticed that old familiar glint of mischief in Isaac's eye: the hustle. So, of course, Isaac did his thing, made it seem like this novel idea had just occurred to him, something we could all do together and have a little fun at. He made his move. He offered his cousins an opportunity to make some money and at the same time give our guest, meaning me, a real taste of how basketball runs like blood through the veins of this family. He even sweetened the pot by letting the cousins who were three in number play against just the two of us. Well, it took about two seconds for the cousins to jump at the idea and be well on their way towards a payday. So they thought. The four cousins were after all close, knew each other's game, and were all up for a good laugh.

We headed over to the park adjacent to the high school to a court like I had never seen in my life, never seen in all the schoolyards that I played in up in The Bronx, where you'd be lucky if the pole was straight, the rim was level, and the cement underfoot even. This was a full court with an unknown softer surface on the ground, not exactly cement, and not exactly pavement. All I knew was that it was easier on your feet. And the hoop, well if I had had a ruler I'm sure it was regulation height and if I had had a level, perfectly straight. The backboard was also made of a thick white plastic material that I had never seen before. It had markings to show the shooter the sweet spots for a bank shot. And it was solid. It didn't budge. Sometimes back home, a loose rim helped the ball go in, but don't bet on it. It was a full court, with all the professional markings of a key, the foul line, out-of-bounds line, and half court. Back home, your pocket comb, or a set of keys or a soda bottle or spit would be your markers. This was the big time.

I took Isaac on the side and asked, "What? Are you crazy? We haven't played in years."

Calm, cool, and collected as always, he answered, "Steve, don't worry about it. Once you got it—and my brother, we got it—you never lose it. Just run the plays, Steve." As always, I listened, heard, agreed, and chilled out.

"No problem with the three on two?" I asked.

"Steve, just run the plays."

"Okay, boss," I said. "Let's play!"

Damn! It was like heaven on earth! There we were, back and better than ever. Fake the lay-up, no-look pass to Isaac under the hoop, boom, he lays it right in. Next play, same thing again, except we faked them out. I moved to the baseline, Isaac hits me with a behind-the-head no-look pass, I nail the jumper, swish, nothing but net. Just as a reminder, unlike The Bronx, these hoops actually had nets. We went like that for two games. The first one, we won by five and the second one, once we got warmed up, we shut them out.

Isaac was beaming, as was I. He kept ribbing his three cousins about the lead in their feet and how out of shape they were. After the surprise of the literal assault and the amazing finely tuned arsenal of our offense, not to mention several blocks by Isaac and a few of my steals, they could do nothing but laugh and scratch their heads in awe. In their own right, the cousins were all good ball players. But, me and Isaac were magic. Always were.

Terry went and got us some orange Fanta sodas and we all sat down on a bench to take a breather. While me and Isaac were giving his cousins some background about our illustrious hustling career up in The Bronx, we saw a group of teenage boys come through the gate down on the other end of the full court. There were five of them and one was dribbling a basketball. When I turned around I noticed Isaac and the cousins had stopped laughing. They had stopped talking. I glanced over at Isaac and saw a shadow pass over his face. He wasn't smiling. His eyes were focused on the five guys at the other end of the court. The three cousins, uneasiness on their faces, were also tracking the movements of the five guys. All five guys were white.

One minute me and Isaac had been reminiscing about our escapades. We had the cousins literally belly laughing. But the next minute, dead silence and gloom. I couldn't figure it out. It all happened instantaneously, in mid-sentence.

The guy with the ball dropped it at his buddy's feet and swaggered over to us, a smirk on his face. I started to feel the hair on the back of my neck get all prickly. It was trouble. I just wasn't sure what kind. Automatically, my fist clenched. Isaac gave me a nudge. I looked up at him and he shook his head. He knew I was tough, maybe a tad overreactive. The guy gave me the once-over and snickered. He turned back to his boys and one gave him a nod. Then the guy turned back to us, and with his eyes on the cousins, he said, "You niggas are gonna play ball with us. And you white boy, what the fuck is wrong with you?" There went my fist again. Isaac, right next to me, put his hand on the front of my forearm to restrain me. Bernard, his eyes cast downward, said softly, "Yes sir, sure, we'll play you." I had all I can do to contain myself, but I knew Isaac wanted me to keep my cool. So I did. The kid went back to his guys and gave them a thumbs up. They started warming up on their end of the court.

The cousin's eyes were downcast and they were shuffling their feet. I turned to Isaac and asked, "What the fuck is goin' on here?" Isaac had that look that I saw when he had guided me out of the projects that day when Dr. King got shot. I saw fear, resignation, rage—all at once. I was starting to understand but it didn't fully take hold until we began to play.

These white kids took the ball up first. In truth, they could hardly dribble. They were awkward. They committed all kinds of basic violations like double dribbling, traveling, and palming the ball. When I was about to open my mouth to make the calls, Isaac put his finger to his lips and motioned for me to keep quiet. I was fuming and was having a hell of a time controlling myself. So, instead of making the call, I ran over and easily stole the ball from the white guys. I started bringing it upcourt, but seeing how none of my guys got open or seemed to want to play any offense, I scored an easy layup. This went on a few more times, me being a one-man team with no one to pass the ball to. My guys, my team, were getting more and more reluctant to play ball.

These white guys sucked and I was thinking, *Let's make them pay for their bullshit attitudes.* The next time I took the ball up, one of the white guys deliberately tripped me. I lost the ball and they scored. My guys provided no defense. The next time a guy punched me in the shoulder. They scored again. No defense.

The white boys were laughing and feeling proud of themselves. Isaac didn't let me handle the ball for two more possessions and deliberately lost it, turning it over to the white guys. I was fit to be tied, furious. I felt like I was in the *Twilight Zone.* Finally, we had possession and the score was 4–3, their favor. I glanced over at Isaac who was barely jogging up the court while Dwayne was making believe he didn't know how to dribble. I yelled at

Isaac, "What's wrong with you man? Let's get these guys! Let's beat the piss out of them, they stink and we're just fuckin' around here!" Isaac, sad and resigned, quietly told me, "We have to let them win." I saw his mouth moving, but it was like he was speaking Chinese or something. I said to myself, *Did I just hear what I thought I heard?* We never *let* anybody win. Sure, we lost our share of games, but it wasn't because we ever let anybody win. I stared at my buddy, my brother, and I just wanted to cry. I looked over to the cousins who were feigning stupidity. I saw these ignorant, arrogant, white, terrible basketball players laughing and congratulating themselves up and down the court.

The game, thankfully, went to only five because the white boys were winded. Me and my guys went back to the bench we had been sitting on before. All five of the white boys came over to the bench this time. The guy who had first come over to us laughed and said, "When you niggas gonna learn? And you, white boy, you are no better than them. Better not let me catch you alone." I threw down the ball, jumped up off the bench, and went for him. I was going to kill him. My whole crew restrained me. The white boys sauntered off, shaking their heads laughing.

All the rest of that day and the next, it being my last full day before I went home, I didn't talk much. Ma tried to feed me pork chops to cheer me up. Yvonne and Yvette tried to get me going by tickling and teasing me. Isaac couldn't or wouldn't look me in the eye. I barely saw the cousins. My mood shifted 180 degrees. After my anger subsided, I started to figure it all out just like Mr. Gordon had warned: Delaware is the South. It's a different set of rules. Now, what to do about my feelings?

My world was shattered, upside down and backwards. Isaac, the Isaac I so loved and admired and respected and needed, had basically vanished. No more laughing and joking. He had the same body, but it was as if his spirit had been sucked right out of him. Two years ago, if this had been me and Isaac in The Bronx, we would have beat their asses on and off the court. Instead this Isaac said, "We have to let them win."

The Isaac I knew back in The Bronx was quick to laugh, never backed down, was prideful and strong. But, the Isaac I saw after the so-called game with the white boys, was hardly a shadow of the old Isaac.

I couldn't reconcile it all. Nice house, trees, grass, a nice car, nice basketball court but so what? In exchange for what? Your soul? That's how it felt.

The next morning it was time for me to go home. I had my bag packed, the taxi was blowing its horn, and everyone lined up outside by the side door to give me a hug and wish me well. I did my best to smile and thank everybody for their hospitality as I moved down the good-bye line. Isaac was last. He shook my hand and our eyes locked for a brief moment. A tear rolled down his cheek. We embraced. We weren't smiling. No words were spoken. I waved a final good-bye to everybody, got in the cab, and turned back as I watched my Delaware family wave good-bye to me.

From the Wilmington station, I took the train and then the subway and got off seven hours later on 167th Street and the Grand Concourse. I walked the four blocks to my apartment. No trees. No grass. Cement, honking cars, moms and their babies, dogs barking, noise, large brick buildings, and that unmistakable Bronx stench in the air—dog shit and fumes. As I walked home, I was thinking that no matter how bad this Bronx is, it is so much better than Delaware.

I never saw Isaac again. One year later, as a senior graduating from DeWitt Clinton High School, I felt the urge to go back to Nelson Avenue to connect with and touch something of my life with Isaac. I was moving on in the world and I was feeling nostalgic. I didn't know what my future held in store for me. On the one hand, I was feeling excited but on the other hand I was scared of losing the good stuff. Isaac was the good stuff, at least the Isaac I knew on Nelson Avenue back in the day.

When I got to Nelson Avenue, I saw Tyrone, a kid who me and Isaac had known. Tyrone was leaning up against the now boarded-up Klein's butcher shop where I used to work. His eyes were watering and glazed over. He was having trouble holding his head up. He was scratching his face and rubbing his nose. Tyrone was coming down off a heroin high and looked like shit. I went up to him and asked him if he heard anything from Isaac. When his eyes finally focused and Tyrone realized it was me standing in front of him, he smiled wanly and asked me for money. I emptied out my pockets and gave him what I had. He thought for a second and then said, slurring his words, "Yeah, man. Guys up the block said Isaac was a boxer, tryin' out for the Olympics." Sure enough, I was able to confirm Tyrone's information with the guys up the block. They told me Isaac had made the cut.

Teary-eyed, I peered beyond the rooftops through the smog and haze at the perfectly cloudless blue sky, and then, as I lowered my head, my eyes came to rest on a pigeon pecking at an old dried up sandwich on the sidewalk. I took a deep breath, lifted my gaze, looked around the old neighborhood, and smiled.

CHAPTER FOUR

ALL SHARKS, NO JETS

Amy took one look at me and started to tear up. I was sitting on our stoop, my dungarees were ripped, I had a black eye and my lip was bloody. My whole body ached from the beating. You'd think a fourteen-year-old kid, bleeding, all beat up, and sitting alone on a stoop would get some sympathy, at least some kind of attention. Nothing. And there were plenty of people passing by. I wasn't looking for it, but it would have been nice.

I told you 1968 was the year of my first real girlfriend, but it was also the year of the worst beating of my life.

Amy used her shirtsleeve to wipe away a tear. Me and Amy had learned that shit happens. We didn't overreact. We barely reacted at all. We moved on real quick.

My eyes were fixed on the gooey, melting bubble gum spots on the sidewalk in front of me. Sirens were blaring in the background a couple of blocks away, and the street sweeper trucks were doing their thing spraying water and swishing garbage and dog shit all over the place with their giant brushes. I hardly noticed any of it. I just sat there in my own world of hurt clutching my basketball.

My sister, Amy, had just gotten back from taking her SAT test. For the last few weeks she had been studying like crazy. I hadn't seen her this energetic about anything in so long.

Three weeks earlier, about midnight, I had gotten out of bed to pee. When I flipped on the light, the cock-roaches all split and when my eyes came into focus, I saw Amy sitting there at the dining room table with a flashlight feverishly going through the SAT practice tests. She looked up at me and I whispered, "What's goin' on, Ame?"

"I gotta get out of this fucking madhouse, away from this. Away from them. We can't even walk the streets, he's a fucking, drunken maniac and she's a pathetic child. All I gotta do now is get good grades on this test. I slept through the last three years of high school and having crappy grades is the same no matter what high school you come from. Bronx Science doesn't do me any good on paper. So this is it for me. Most of my friends either have money or scholarships. I got shit. I'll go to City College if I have to, but I gotta get away. Here, test me on these vocab words."

For the last few weeks I had helped her with vocabulary for an hour a night until her test that Saturday morning.

And now, here we were on the stoop. Amy was making her first real move to get out. And me, I was recovering from the worst beating I ever got.

She was all decked out in tight, cuffed jeans, a tank top and she had her usual denim shirt tied at her waist. Makeup, the whole works. Even her hair was looking good, a short shag haircut, like Goldie Hawn wore on *Laugh-In.*

Evidently this test was a big deal and she had dressed up for it. I asked how the test had gone. She didn't say anything for a few seconds. Her eyes were wet and she took her gaze from me to the street and then back to me and said, "You remember one of those times mom took Richard and went up to Grampa's to take care of him? The time you told me you thought she was gonna jump out the window?"

"Yeah, Ame, it was when we were living up in the projects. Mom was standing next to the window, crying. In one hand she had her suitcase, and the other hand was on the window handle. I begged her to take us away."

"Well, do you remember there was that one time, dad wasn't drunk and it was a Saturday, and he took us to the movies? You know, across the bridge in the Spanish neighborhood where he took us for rice and beans after? You remember, Steve."

I nodded my head, all fogged up not only from the beating I just took but from trying to remember what seemed so long ago. I think I had been six or seven at the time. "Oh yeah, the story about the Puerto Rican girl and the white guy and they fell in love and the gangs. Downtown, right, Ame?"

"Yeah, Steve, maybe you were too young but I loved that movie. Romantic. Those two really, really loved each other. I mean they really loved each other!! I never thought true love was possible until I saw that movie. And the music! You remember the dancing and the singing?"

"Oh yeah, in the gym? Right, Ame? The gangs wanted to fight. Sharks and Jets. Puerto Ricans and white guys."

"Yeah, Steve. Not just in the gym. All the time. You remember the scene when the gang leaders got killed, the rumble, and then at the end Tony dies in the playground and Maria is left holding him? That broke my heart. I don't know if you remember but the fighting was about the two of them, mostly. Their love. But not only. Their love for each other brought out the hate in everybody else."

After a few seconds, she looked right into my eyes. Her voice grew louder and faster, almost screaming. She asked, "You got beat up, didn't you? They came after you again, didn't they?" Then more softly, "I see it in your eyes when you're with Elaine. I never had that. I wish I did. Steve, it's just like the movie. It's just like *West Side Story*. Bronx style. Maria and Tony, you and Elaine. It's the same thing! She's Puerto Rican, you're white. The Puerto Ricans keep picking on you and now beating you. They don't want a white boy with one of theirs. It is so much the same! How you two love each other, how you can't think of anything else, how happy you are, even in this pile of shit we live in, when you are with her or just telling me about her! I'm happy for you. But look at you, you're a mess! What happened? Where were your friends? Were you alone? Do you know who jumped you? Is it worth all this? Seems like every day it's something else. They threaten. They hit. And now, this. Is it worth it?"

"Ame! Stop! Listen to me. I love her so much! I would die for her! I get these feelings around her that anything is possible. I can do anything! You've seen me. I feel like Superman. I walk around with a smile now. When did we ever smile? You hear me. I tell you how beautiful she is and I dream about her at night. I go down the block to the schoolyard making believe I'm gonna play basketball, just hoping to get a glimpse of her looking for me from her window across the street. Just that alone is enough. It makes this shitty life magic, a dream. I have hope now that I have Elaine. Is it worth it? I'd pay this price a million times.

"I hear you about *West Side Story*. This is not that! If this Bronx was downtown and I could sing and dance, *maybe* I could see it. Oh yeah, there's gangs, Ame. But, up here in The Bronx in this neighborhood, it's all Sharks, no Jets. No Jets, just me. Even if there were Jets, I wouldn't be one. I don't have hate; I just want to love Elaine. I'm always alone. They cornered me. All I got is how much I love her."

Amy sat down. More tears. Both of us now. Amy dried her eyes and looked at me and said, "I didn't take the test. I got the wrong date. It's next Saturday. But at least I'm ready."

"I'll help you more any night you need, Ame."

"Thanks. I got all year to figure out college. This is the first step," she said. "I'm getting out. I'm going crazy. I worry he's going to kill one of us some day. I watch you doing what you do to protect us. You distract him, you do whatever he tells you so he doesn't come after us. You tell Richard how to avoid him. You move him along to the bedroom to be out of sight when Dad comes home. You make sure Mom is okay so she doesn't need too much. You walk her to work, you walk her home, you give her money. Steve, when I get myself together I'll come back for you. Maybe I'll get married. Whatever. We'll get Richard some help. Real help. I just gotta get into college so I can get a good job and get us the fuck out.

"Maureen, you know my red-haired girl friend? She needs a place to stay. Her dad is a drunk and beats her. And other stuff. I'm gonna let her stay with me in my room."

"Is our place any better?" I asked. "Our dad is no prince, Ame."

"Yeah, but hers is doing bad things to her. At least our dad never messed with me like that. Sometimes, I thought he was going to, but no. They'll hardly know she's there. I'll keep it low key."

"All good," I said. "I like Maureen. She's pretty."

Marcus came out of his building and sheepishly walked by my stoop, hanging his head, eyes on the sidewalk. Marcus was the kid from down south. First week here, I reached out to him. He said I was his first white friend. Marcus was a little shorter than me. Same age, kind of light skinned and pudgy with a big blocky head. He was wearing his blue suede Playboys, his silk T-shirt, and his blue sharkskin pants. He walked with a prance like the rest of the Black guys in the neighborhood. I thought we were tight. Until that day. I didn't even look at him. Amy right away picked up on it and said to him, "Some fucking friend you are. Look what happened to my brother. What'd you do, run away? Did all of you run away and leave him there to die? You fucking coward. Why? Is it because he's white?"

Marcus said, "Yo, that was Frankie and Robert's boys. They killers. We weren't sticking around for that shit. They after Gog, not us. He shouldn't be messin' with that Spanish girl." Marcus moved on, eyes cast downward, eager to be out of our company.

"Steve, tell me what happened. Didn't you work today?"

"Yeah, so there was nothing happenin' on the jobs for me so I stayed in the shop and cleaned it up. I put all the plumbing shit away from the last few weeks work and organized the brass and cast iron. That was it. I was done at around one. So, I went down to the schoolyard, lookin' like I was lookin' for a game, but what I was really lookin' for was Elaine lookin' out her window lookin' for me."

"Wow! That's a lotta lookin'! What's all that about?" Amy asked.

"Well, I know it sounds stupid but in reality, we don't see each other that much. I'm always at school or workin' or takin' care of Richard, and her mom is very strict since the neighborhood got so bad. She makes Elaine stay in a lot, so sometimes all we got is just that. She sits there in her window up on the fifth floor in that building across the street from the schoolyard and I catch quick glances of her watching me. It's like electricity when our eyes connect. I can feel it! Seeing her makes all the difference as to whether my day will be good or bad, whether I'll be happy or sad, whether dad's bullshit will drag me down or I'll be able to let it go."

Amy asked, "The schoolyard's on the corner, which building you talkin' about?"

"If you stood under the hoop, with your back towards the foul line, well, if there was a foul line, instead we use chalk or keys, mostly spit, to mark off the foul line and outta bounds lines, and then you looked out towards McClellan Street and kind of look right a little bit to where the bodega is and then you look up to the fifth floor of the building there and then you see the fire escape and just to the right of the fire escape is Elaine's bedroom window."

"Got it. That's 225 McClellan. I knew some guys down the block from there," Amy said.

"You did? Who?"

"Don't matter," she said.

"So, anyways, I get to the opening in the fence goin' in to the school yard and shot a look up to her window and saw a sheet or a blanket covering it up from the inside. Ame, I just went down the tubes. I was looking forward to seeing her so much!

"I saw the guys playin', Marcus and Skip and Dee and Allie were all there, playin' two-on-two. Karl was cheerleading off to the side using his cane with the African head on it. It seemed like they were havin' fun and I was feelin' so down since Elaine wasn't in her window. You know, usually when I hear the ball bounce or I hear it clunk off the rim, I get this charge, you know like a real shot goes through me. Not today. I was just hoping to see Elaine. Could care less about basketball today. So, I forced myself to go in and call 'next.'

"Ame, I gotta ask you somethin' else. About a week ago, the guys were teasing me about Elaine."

"Whaddya mean?"

"Well, we were out in front of Skip's stoop on Sherman the other day and Elaine passed by on the other side of the street. As I started to cross over to talk to her, they all started snickering and saying shit to each other, quiet like.

"When I got back from talking to her, Skip said, 'Gog! You the man! Gimme five. I bet you love gettin' into all that,' and he was checkin' Elaine out as she passed by."

Amy asked, "What was she wearing?"

"Well, you know, you've seen her, she got those tight, blue, cutoff shorts and her shirt was," Amy broke in and asked, "That black silky top she wore when I met her?"

"Yeah," I said.

"Steve, Elaine is fucking beautiful. They're jealous, that's all."

"Yeah, but what did they mean by 'gettin' into all that?' I didn't know if I should feel happy, mad, proud, what? I never even kissed her."

"Yeah. It's all good, Steve. You love each other, that's the main thing. Don't listen to them. I'll have a talk with Skip."

"No, Ame, that's alright."

Just then Louis walked by. Louis was cool. A Puerto Rican guy, lived in the building, in his twenties, worked downtown somewhere, usually had a suit and tie on, carried a briefcase and had on a pair of brown leather Playboys. But, today instead of the suit, he had on a tan knit shirt and a leather beret. He was tall and dark skinned, like Elaine, and had a goatee. My sister lit up. He looked over and smiled when he saw us. Amy said in a real sweet way, "Oh, hello, Louis, so nice to see you again," as she flashed him a big smile.

I don't know what happened, but something came over me. I snapped. I slammed the basketball down, jumped up off the stoop and tackled Louis to the ground, pummeling him. Louis was a good fighter, but he didn't hit me. From underneath me, he bear-hugged me, and easily rolled me over onto my back. With his weight now on top of me, he kept my arms pinned onto the sidewalk. Amy screamed at me, "Steve, stop! Louis is a good guy!"

I was in a blind rage, but with Amy screaming and Louis immobilizing me, I calmed down. Louis let go of his hold on me as we stood up. Amy told Louis she was sorry and told him she'd catch up to him later. He brushed himself off, was all puzzled, and went into the building.

"What the fuck was that, Steve?"

"I dunno know what happened."

"I thought you said you didn't have hate!"

"Ame, I don't, you know I don't."

"Well what was that? Is it because he's a P.R.?"

"No! It's you. You deserve better, the best."

"He's just someone I know from the building, Steve. A nice guy."

"Yeah, but the two of you looked at each other in a way that made me crazy. Ame, I want the best for you. I don't know what came over me. The white thing, the Puerto Rican thing, you seeming like you like him, me getting the shit kicked out of me because of Elaine, all the shit at home, my boys leavin' me hangin'. All of it and then us. Our life. Can't go out at night. The junkies always coming after us. For what? Pennies, loose change? They kill for that. Then there's fuckin' Frankie and Robert sellin' their dope and makin' sure that me the only white kid around here is not doin' anything with a Spanish girl. And then there's us. Our fucked-up parents. Really, Ame, we're the parents. Mom is always crying and telling me her problems, mainly about Dad. He's the problem. They both are. You know my old friend Isaac, from back in our old neighborhood? Well, I saw Isaac's mom kick his stepfather out of the apartment more than once because he was drunk. We don't get that. We got a mom who tells us how great our father is. Fuck! He's a drunk, he yells and screams at us and makes us feel like shit all the time. He makes us ashamed. He's crazy and she goes along with it."

Amy kept nodding her head yes and then said, "Yeah, I know, Steve, it's all fucked up. You don't have to worry about Louis. I'm still seeing Mike. You remember, the sailor guy who gave you Wolf?"

"Yeah," I said. Just her mentioning Wolf's name hit me hard. "Wolf! He was the greatest. I miss him so much."

In my foggy and throbbing head, I was remembering Wolf.

He'd been gone for a few months by then. I was down. Sad. I loved that dog so much and for him to go the way he did just about killed me. I couldn't get over losing him. At corners, I looked for him, left and right. I would feel him behind me. I'd turn and he'd be gone. In my head, I replay over and over again that night I went to the shop looking for him. The leash, collar, and bowl on the floor. No Wolf. Then Jimmie, that fucking piece of shit with that beer can in that bag and that cigarette hanging out his mouth with his front teeth crooked and brown and him leaning against the shop window smiling, smirking, when he told me, "It was your daddy, he lost him in a card game." And my old man, drunk with a bottle of scotch dangling from his hand, out cold, snoring on the cot in the shop. That night replayed over and over again. Then me, frantic, looking for Wolf in the alleys, basements, schoolyard. All the fun me and Wolf had. The day he saved my life. All of it. Over and over again for months, in my head. Couldn't sleep. Couldn't cry. Couldn't focus on school. Like a zombie. And then the clouds lifted. The sun came out. Even before I met Elaine, I started feeling like something good was coming. It had to. I couldn't live like that anymore. And then, there she was.

"Yeah," Amy said, "I was sad, too. I loved how you loved that dog. I loved how he perked up when he heard your keys jangling in the locks on the shop door, as you would yell out, "Wolf, get up. Let's go!" He even wagged his tail. Before that he was just a big lazy mutt. That's why Mike had to get rid of him. He was not a good watchdog on the boat when they docked and needed stuff guarded."

"Yeah. So, life got better and then, pow! My girl appeared in my life. I been walkin' on air, Ame."

"So, first tell me what happened just now with Louis and then tell me about the fight."

"You know, I don't know. Maybe it is the Puerto Rican thing, maybe it's because I worry about you and want you to be happy and nobody is gonna be good enough for you. Maybe it's watchin' you making plans to move out. Maybe after today, I'm all fucked up. Can you tell Louis I'm sorry?"

"You tell him yourself," she said. "He's a good guy, he'll get it. He's got a sister he worries about too," she said.

"So yeah, anyway after I called 'next,' the guys finished up their game. When I started playin', a gang of Puerto Ricans came into the schoolyard. My boys scattered. I'm still not sure who runs this neighborhood, the Black guys like in my gang, or the Puerto Ricans. Sure ain't us, Ame. I don't know if you know them but the brothers, Frankie and Robert, run that gang, and this neighborhood. I don't get it, Ame, they're whiter than we are. They more than anybody are always after me. They act and talk Spanish and have babies with their Spanish girlfriends. Frankie and Robert are always saying how they're gonna fuck me up, the white boy, and whitey this and whitey that."

Amy said, "Wait a second. I know who you mean. Louis was telling me about them one day. Louis used to hang out with them when they were younger. They live down on 166th. They're bad fuckin' news, Steve. Louis said they got some kind of chip on their shoulder because their dad, who was Italian, left them and their mom, who was Puerto Rican, when they were little. They grew up hating white people and were always gettin' into trouble, startin' fights, gettin' kicked out of school and are all around just bad. They're into heroin and bad shit. Stay clear of them."

"They came after me. They're always pickin' on me. Shit about how I can't be with any Puerto Rican girls in *their* neighborhood. Always comin' after me. Especially after I been on the street with Elaine.

"The last time was when I was playing basketball about a week ago. It was Robert on his own—no Frankie—and a couple of his boys who came into the schoolyard while I was just shootin' around by myself, sneaking looks up at Elaine's window. Robert said, 'Let's play, white boy.'

"I knew it was gonna be trouble. Elaine was not in her window right then. She told me later if she saw I was in trouble she woulda come right down and kicked their ass."

"I believe her," Amy said.

"I was not about to play ball with those guys. All it would be is a reason to pin me down and beat me. So, I said no, picked up my ball and started makin' my way to the street. Robert got in my face, slapped the ball out of my hand, and socked me hard in the chest, as his boys circled me. He asked, 'What the fuck? You too good for us?' The punch hurt, Ame. You woulda been proud of me. I picked up my ball and tried to move out of the schoolyard again. Again, he got in my face and pushed me back. You seen him right, Ame? He's this short little white guy. And he's got all these Spanish guys around him. So I stared right into his gray eyes, took a quick scan of the gang, and then shot a glance up to Elaine's empty window. I said, 'I'll tell you what. Me and you. Just us.' I was calm. I was fuckin' mad and I had had it by then. Lookin' up for Elaine made me strong."

"So what happened?" Amy asked.

"Robert took a second and said, 'No, I'm not doin' that, and moved out of my way. I picked up my ball and calmly walked towards the opening in the fence. To my back he yelled, 'Watch your step, white boy!'"

"Wow! You were lucky, Steve!"

"I don't think so, Ame. It gave him time to plan the next attack. This one today. He was probably pissed off and felt like a coward in front of his boys when I made him back down."

"So what happened today, Steve?"

"This time it was both brothers, Frankie and Robert, and their other guys, too. My guys took one look and ran off."

"Fucking cowards," Amy said.

"Yeah, but it's more than that, Ame. We're white. Look around, we're the only white people left in the neighborhood."

"Yeah," Amy said, "but you'd swear by lookin' at 'em, those two pieces of shit were white, too."

"Yeah, I know, Ame. It don't make sense. So, Frankie had a bat. The other guys yanked me over to that little space to the side of the hoop, it's a little area between the two parts of the school building. You can't see it from the street. They cornered me. They punched and kicked me and then Frankie took a swing at my knees with the bat. I went down. Ame, my knees are killin' me."

"They look bad, Steve."

"Robert just watched. And smiled. The whole thing took about five minutes. Lucky they didn't hit my head, they woulda killed me."

"No, Steve," Amy said. "They knew just what they were doin'. That's murder. This was a beating. They were teachin' you a lesson. Can't learn if you're dead and besides, word would get around and they'd get put away for a long time. They know the ropes."

"While I was getting hit, Frankie kept yelling, 'You want a P.R. girl? This is what it gets you, motha' fucker. This is what you get! You hear me, white boy?' And he swung and they kicked. They ground my face into the sidewalk. There was glass from broken beer bottles. See the cuts?"

"Yeah, Steve."

"Then they split. All four of them went different directions, left the bat. I almost cried, Ame. I was so hurt, in so much pain, bleeding, so confused. Why should love hurt so bad? Why should it have to be so fuckin' hard to be happy?"

"Story of our life, isn't it?" she said. "So, all this happened when? Around one or two you said?"

"Yeah, something like that."

"Well, it's four now. Whatchu been doin' for the last couple of hours? Not just sitting here, I hope?"

It was getting late. People on the street were starting to hang out in front of their buildings, sitting on their stoop or a folding chair, drinking beer, playing cards or dominos on little fold-up card tables or milk crates. Some of the guys kept their little transistor radios close to their ears, listening to the Yankee game. Little boys were playing stickball in the street and the little girls were on the sidewalk, skipping rope Double Dutch. Another Saturday night on the block. Me and Amy hardly noticed.

"Yeah, Ame, I guess I've been sitting here a while. After I got beat up, I got up off the cement and started making my way out of the schoolyard when Mr. Rivera saw me. You know the guy who owns the bodega on the corner of Sherman?"

"Yeah. I like him, he's always so nice," Amy said. "Hey, isn't Mr. Rivera Hector's dad, your friend who drowned?"

"Yeah."

"He's a nice man. Sad," Amy said. "Hey, what happened? You never really got into it? Weren't you there when it happened, when Hector drowned?"

"Yeah, I was. I just couldn't think about it and didn't wanna talk about it. Me and Hector and a couple other guys went up to The High Bridge, up the E. L. Grant Highway, near where we used to live in the projects. Ame, you remember, the High Bridge, that old dilapidated bridge that connects The Bronx to Manhattan?"

"Yeah," she said. "It runs alongside the Cross Bronx."

"Yeah. The High Bridge was where sometimes me and Isaac used to go to jump off some rocks on the real hot days and swim around in the Harlem River.

"Steve, I never knew that!"

"I know, I didn't think it would go over too good. It's all slimy and stinky and shit would be floating all around. But on the real scorching days at least it was wet. See, Ame, it was me who brought Hector to the High Bridge. He never knew about it before. That was his first time jumping in, the day he drowned. I couldn't get it out of my head. First him jumping in and never coming up and then me, the one who brought him there."

"I never knew any of this, Steve."

"Yeah, I know. I been holdin' it in. I feel so guilty. It was hot that day and me and Hector bumped into each other down at the bodega. I was on my third Mavi. You know what Mavi is, right Ame?"

"Mavi, what the fuck is that?"

"It's like Puerto Rican root beer. Elaine introduced me to it. Real good. I'll get you one.

"Usually, on the hot days, I get the big monkey wrench out of the shop or van and turn on the hydrant for everyone to cool off in. That is, until the cops or fire department come and shut it down. Well, the wrench wasn't in the shop and the van was nowhere to be found. So, when I told Hector I knew a place, not too far to go swimmin', he said, 'Take me, bro, it's so hot!' So, we went. He never came back. He jumped in with the rest of us and never came up. I ran out and got the cops. I ran down to 169th where the 44th Precinct was."

Amy said, "You must have remembered where that precinct was from way back when your bike got stolen. I remember tellin' you to go down there and file a report."

"Yeah, never got that bike back, though. Or any of the rest of them for that matter. So what happened was, cops came, fire department came, ambulance, everything. They found Hector and pulled him out. The cops didn't let us see him. They put something like a sheet around him. They kept us there, asked us a bunch of questions, and then they drove us back to the neighborhood in their cruiser. The other guys, Hector's friends, went to see his family at the bodega. I came home. I shoulda told you about it, Ame, but I just felt so sad and guilty."

"So, Mr. Rivera helped you today?"

"Yeah, he brought me into the back of the store and put plastic bags of ice on my knees and cleaned me up. You know what? You know what he said to me? I can't get over it. He thanked me. He told me how happy he was that Hector and me became friends. The neighborhood was goin' down, he said. He remembers when there were more white people, no drugs, and very little crime. He said at one time it was a good place to live. He asked, 'Frankie and Robert did this, didn't they? They don't want you hangin' around with that cute *chica* across the street, right?' Then he said, 'I know, it's been all over the neighborhood about you and her. All good stuff. People around here like you, they know you're a good kid. Those *pendejos*, Frankie and Robert, sell their shit to the kids around here, they should both die. What those fools don't know is that they're as white as you are. Who cares what color anybody is, or where they come from or who's Spanish and who's Black or white?' Ame, Mr. Rivera sounds like us. He said, 'This should never have happened. Knees look pretty bad. Use a lot of ice.' He told me that the day his son drowned, the cops had brought Hector's friends to the bodega. They told Mr. Rivera that I was the one who showed everybody the swimming spot under the High Bridge. His family doesn't blame me. His son was gonna do what he was gonna do. And still Mr. Rivera was so nice to me, Ame. He told me his daughters both liked me, too. They were working the register and stocking shelves and he introduced me to them, Alma and Natalie. You know who they are, Ame?"

"Not sure."

"They said hi to me and smiled and Alma, the younger sister, about sixteen, said to come over some time. Natalie invited me to a meeting. I told her, 'Sure, great. What kind of meeting?' 'It's for Father Gigante, he's running to be Bronx councilman and he's our pastor so we gotta support him and attend services.' I asked, 'What kind of services?' Ame, I thought to myself all we ever knew was services at the synagogue and it's already over a year since my bar mitzvah. I haven't set foot in one of those since."

Amy said, "Be careful, Steve. This is gettin' kinda weird."

"I know, Ame, but I feel like I need to do something for these people."

She said, "I get it. Just watch the religious shit. I saw some Puerto Ricans driving around with this giant billboard strapped to the top of a car with a loud microphone with Spanish music, singing and yelling, telling everybody to vote for Father Gigante. I think I saw the word *Pentecostal* or something like that on the car. Don't ask me, I have no idea what that is. I barely understand our own religion half the time."

"Yeah. I'll be careful, Ame. So, I hung down at the bodega with Mr. Rivera for a while and then limped up here and been just sitting here on the stoop, depressed. What a fucking day, huh?"

"Yeah, we'll get through it. Get upstairs and clean up before you get questions about all your bruises. I'll sneak some towels and stuff in to you. You gotta think about hangin' around with some better people, Steve."

"I'm tryin', Ame."

"Yeah, I know you are."

It was getting late. We had been talking for over an hour. We hardly ever had that kind of time together. It's always on the go, trying to avoid home as much as possible and get through the days. She was always with her boyfriend or school friends, sometimes she didn't even come home at night. Now she's making plans to move out and I'm trying to figure out how to survive.

"So," she said, "you know, you never did tell me how you and Elaine met. How'd that happen?" Amy sat next to me and smiled, ready for the story. Even Amy's hair was lookin' good, a telltale sign that she was on top of her game. When shit was hitting the fan in her life, usually our old man picking on her, she started pulling from her eyebrows first, then her eyelashes, then her head. I was so proud sitting on our stoop with my beautiful sister.

I was starting to forget about my bruises and lightened up when I thought about Elaine. All the hubbub in the street faded away as I told Amy how me and Elaine met. It felt real good to be sharing this time with Amy in this way. We really got closer that day on the stoop. I knew she'd always be there for me.

"Well, Ame, it's funny how you say I better find some better guys to hang out with. There is this one guy. His name is Mikey or Morty or Fish. Or, all three of them. He's just about the only other white kid around. He lives a couple blocks down, near Morris Avenue. He's the one who introduced us.

"Wait a second, why does he have three names?" she asked.

"He works down at his dad's fish store on 167th. It's called Morty's. So, on the street he's known as Mikey, his real name, but when the guys tease him and say he smells like fish, they call him Morty or Fish. You remember the time a few months ago when all I had to protect me against that gang was Wolf. Anyway, Mikey, believe

119

it or not, was the only person who, even though it was hours later, came up here to this stoop to ask if I needed any help when that gang was after me. The only one!"

"Wow, I didn't know that," Amy said. "He sounds like a good kid."

"Yeah, too bad he's movin' to Staten Island."

"Too bad," she said. "You need a friend like that."

"Yeah, so, he introduced me and Elaine."

For the next half hour I told Amy most of the story, or at least that part of it which got cleared up when me and Elaine reconnected and met up back at the neighborhood forty-five years later. Here's the story.

* * *

Morty, Mikey, Fish hooked us up. To keep things manageable, I'm just going to call him Mikey. I was on 167th on my way to the store where the two old Jewish guys sold irregular pants. I needed a new pair of dungarees. The price was always about half of what Alexander's sold them for and the irregular part was usually not too bad. Sometimes the dungarees had a run in the material or sometimes the zipper was stuck. One time a pair came through without back pockets. Stuff like that.

I remember asking one of those old guys where he gets the pants from. With a thick Yiddish accent he went on and on like this: "Well, boychik," he said, "it's not so easy to get beautiful pants like this and to sell them to you so cheap." He told me how he had to go for hours on a train and schlep a big bag every week. He said, "I have to deal with the Chinese and the *shvartzes* and the Mafia down near the river. Every week I go through places where bad people want to cut my throat and take my money and my bag of clothes, just so I can get these beautiful dungarees up to The Bronx, just for you." He wrapped up his spiel with the usual, "Never mind about that, for you, today I have a special deal."

I knew he was really talking about taking the subway down to Delancey on the Lower East Side and haggling with the Jews, buying the pants for a buck and selling them up here for five. He probably stopped in Chinatown for lunch to get some chop suey or maybe Little Italy for some spaghetti.

Well, the irregular pants storefront was right next to Morty's. I took a look into the fish store and saw Mikey. He had rubber gloves on and was wearing a bloodied white apron. He was reaching into a cooler, pulling out big slimy fish and putting them on ice in the display case right in the front window. There were dark ones with whiskers and light ones, almost like silver and gold that my family sometimes ate. As I was passing by, Mikey looked up and waved to me to come in. I hated the smell of fish and it really was quite disgusting to me to see him handling them with their slippery, slimy skin and their dead eyes, cold and black, always seeming to be looking at you wherever you were standing. Mikey was used to it.

He thought nothing of either the smell or their spooky look. I shook my head and pinched my nose, so he took off his gloves and came out to the street to talk.

Just then this beautiful girl with tight denim cut-off shorts and this big wide smile and delicious looking skin like I never saw before came over to talk to Mikey. They knew each other. Mikey and this girl. It wasn't like boyfriend-girlfriend, it was like friends. I kind of went into shock. In a good way. It's good they were talking because I couldn't say anything. My mouth hung open and I know was staring. I couldn't do anything else. I was paralyzed. All I could see was her. The cars going by and their horns blaring, dogs barking, and the hustle and bustle on the sidewalk did not exist. I heard voices, their voices, but it seemed like the sound was coming from another place. Like when you hear people talking from another room in the apartment and you can't make out what they're saying, but you hear their voices. It was just this bubble, this energy field of light around this perfect girl. Nothing else existed. Not even me. That's all there was and it was as close to heaven as I ever felt.

After this amazing girl and her shorts disappeared around the corner, Mikey jabbed me until I came to and he asked, "Gog, whats'a matter? You okay?"

I said, "You kiddin' me? I am happier than I ever been in my life! Who is she? What's her name?"

"That's Elaine, we went to the Deuce together." The Deuce was JHS 22 on Morris Avenue.

I said, "Yo, Mikey I need to get to know her. You gotta introduce me."

He smiled and said, "Fugettaboudit if you're gonna act like you just did."

I wasn't exactly sure what he meant, but I promised, "I'll be good, I'll be cool."

Mikey explained, "Gog, I tried to introduce you but you wouldn't answer. So, I told her you were deaf. Gog, she kept lookin' at you. Did you see her smile? She must really like you. She never smiled like that when it was just me and her. Okay. I'll make it happen."

I was sure I was in love. For the first time in my life, other than with Wolf, I felt joy. Different than I had had with Wolf. This had some other aspects that really intoxicated me.

As much as I loved Wolf, admired him, and had wanted to be with him, play with him, talk to him, make him happy, wrestle with him—all that boy and dog stuff—this was different. Seemed like the same level of feeling, same intensity, but what I wanted was to just be near her. To inhale her.

Sometime that next week, me and Mikey were walking up McClellan Street from the P.S. 90 schoolyard with a couple of Cokes when all of a sudden he stopped short and told me to wait right there. He bolted up the hill and I couldn't quite see where he went, but forty-five years later, Elaine told me what had happened. She said, "Mikey came running up to me and tapped me on the shoulder. He told me that Gog thought I was beautiful and wanted to meet me. When he said your name, he pointed to you down the hill. I smiled ear-to-ear when I realized it was you, the 'deaf' kid, and I said yes! As Mikey was about to turn around and go back down the hill to tell you it was a go, I turned around to head back to the Concourse and I slammed my nose right into one of those red fire department emergency call boxes. I was so embarrassed and I hoped you hadn't seen that. Mikey caught my hand just as I was about to fall and hit the sidewalk. I felt what you felt. Love at first sight."

Sometime that next week, I went down to Elaine's stoop and started talking with her. I'm not going to say I was scared or anything like that, but it was kind of in the same family of scared. I had this fluttering feeling in my chest and stomach, like when something or some-body was after me and I didn't know what was going to happen next but in a good way this time. I felt an excitement like when I was on the basketball court and had just made a great shot. I felt warm all over like I did when I would catch a glimpse of Wolf smiling up at me. I felt like everything was going to be alright like when me and Amy talked or worked out some problem together. All these feelings all at once.

I started going to visit Elaine at her apartment when her parents were home. She lived at 225 McClellan, diagonally across from the schoolyard. I'd be nervous all day anticipating seeing her and then when I finally did, I'd be tongue-tied and clueless. If any of my guys were on the street on the days I went to Elaine's, they would tease me because they'd know I was going because first of all I was clean, and second because I had on my good khakis, a Ban-Lon polo, and my Pro Keds.

Her mom, Maria, was very protective and Elaine hardly ever got out much. Her dad, Pat, seemed so much more laid back and seemed to be always encouraging me to come over more, sit closer to Elaine on the love seat, put my arm around her shoulder, that kind of stuff. He was a cool guy, small and wiry, his hair always slicked back. Pat always had a smoke with a really long ash coming out the end and a can of Rheingold going. He was funny and good natured. He liked me. I think he felt that Elaine would be safe with me. I got the sense he walked on eggshells around his wife and did his best not to cross her. I loved his car, a '64 Plymouth Fury, like the cops had. He painted apartments and Maria worked retail somewhere. She was a beautiful round woman with the same skin as Elaine. Soft and rich, kind of like caramel, good enough to eat I used to think.

Me and Elaine used to sit on the silver brocade love-seat in her living room. Not too much ever happened. I finally got to the point of putting my arm around her and that seemed to make Elaine and Pat very happy. It took me over a month to get that far. All she had to do was smile at me, kind of sideways and I'd melt. I think we both did a good job of holding back, maybe not knowing what we were holding back but the feelings came out between us with a quick glance or a long look, the touch of our skin in our clasped hands, how new and wondrous that sensation was, touching her. I used to dream about that touch. That look. Her skin. Her smile. That new and exciting balled-up feeling swirling around inside. That sweet and exciting combination of softness, warmth, exhilaration, and peacefulness traveling at the speed of light, filling me from my head to my heart to between my legs and back again, whenever we were together. When we weren't together, I still had all that going on but add to that the feeling of dying to see her again. I even felt all that just seeing her in her fifth floor window watching me watching her.

I loved their little dog, Princess. She was a cute black and white Shepard mix, sweet and always eager to play. Sometimes, it was the three of us on the loveseat.

It was summer time. I was working in the plumbing shop. I saved about a 120 bucks for this date I was planning for me and Elaine. A gigantic surprise. First, I went down to the Jewish irregular clothing guys and bought a pair of those new Koratron never-needs-ironing khaki pants and this cool black mesh T-shirt all the guys in the neighborhood were wearing. It showed off your muscles, if you had any. Up on Fordham Road across from Alexander's was a Florsheim shoe store. All the Black and Puerto Rican guys wore Pro Keds, Converse sneakers, or these cool thick, black rubber-soled smooth suede or leather shoes called Playboys. They came in black, brown, or blue. I got me a black pair. That was the first time I ever bought nice clothes for myself. I wanted to look cool for my girl. The clothes and shoes set me back about sixty-five bucks. The rest of the money was for the big surprise that next weekend: Palisades. It looked like heaven from across the river. It was a gigantic amusement park on the New Jersey side of the Hudson.

The TV jingle still plays in my head:

Palisades has the rides,
Palisades has the fun.
Come on over.
Palisades from coast to coast, where a dime buys the most.
Palisades Amusement Park swings all day and after dark.

You couldn't get that song out of your head. It made me happy to think about the Cyclone and the wavy salt water pool and the hot dogs and the cotton candy and the Round-Up and the french fries soaked in vinegar. Best of all, me and Elaine would be off the block, out of the neighborhood, away from the stuff on the street and out from under the parents. That fantasy motivated me to put this unbelievable plan together to get us to Palisades Amusement Park that Saturday.

Here's what I figured out. The week before the date, I did the whole trip by bike to figure out the three buses we'd have to take to get to Palisades. This was the same royal blue Schwinn Continental with the chrome fork that I had bought after my bar mitzvah the year before. Being on that beautiful bike still felt like being on top of the world.

I'll never forget that bike ride. I could have cared less that I had to carry it down eight flights of stairs to the street and then ride about twenty-five city blocks just to get to the bridge to New Jersey. The sun was shining off the water and I flew by, in my own world, happy and excited, cruising by on the walkway of the George Washington Bridge, while all the cars crawled along, stuck in a traffic jam.

So, here's the itinerary. First, we would take the number 35 bus from 167th Street up to the Washington Bridge into Washington Heights. Next, we would walk to the George Washington Bridge and take the bus over the Hudson River and right there at the end of the bridge, we would take the New Jersey Transit bus south, about twenty minutes, straight to the Palisades Amusement Park. By bike, the whole thing took three hours, one way. I checked and wrote down all the bus numbers and the fares and the schedule and laid out the whole trip. To get there was going to take one hour and cost two bucks each. No sweat. I was loaded. With my plumbing apprenticeship I was able to save more than enough to take my girl for the ride of her life.

I went down to Elaine's building around nine in the morning that Saturday and there she was waiting for me on her stoop with her big beautiful smile. All she knew was that there was going to be a surprise, a big one. The weather was perfect and so was she. She was wearing jeans, a blue blouse tied around her waist, and sneakers. Her hair was pulled back and she had on a few bangle bracelets and small hoop earrings. I had on my crisp new slightly irregular Koratron khakis—the belt loops were missing—and my cool shirt and shoes.

As I had planned, we got the three busses and we went across two rivers, first the Harlem River and then the gigantic Hudson River, to a different state. We felt like big shots. We held hands, laughed a lot, and finally made it to the park.

As soon as we pulled into the parking lot and got off the bus, we saw balloons and clowns, heard fireworks and kids laughing, and smelled the popcorn and greasy fries. In the background, against the New York skyline, we saw that white, looming, gigantic, curved monster of a structure called the Cyclone. She seemed to rise up out of the Hudson, climb straight into the clouds like a strange dragon with humps and bumps and a skeleton of white, wooden boards for bones.

The first thing we did was make a bee-line straight to the world-famous Cyclone roller coaster. On that hot Saturday in July, we waited on line for over half an hour with our two twenty-five-cent tickets just to get to the wooden steps leading up to the platform. The line moved slowly as if the hundreds of people on line were being gobbled up by this monster. Her eager victims, locked in with a metal cross bar snapped tight across the chest, four to a car, screaming as she pulled the cars slowly up the first incline, notch by notch. Then, at the top, right when you can see for miles around to both sides of the Hudson, and you get enthralled by the view, she, like a wild and unpredictable serpent, hurls the car straight down. All this as the screams and the roar of her machinery came to a crescendo and she whipped the cars first one way and then another, at sharp almost ninety-degree turns and then up again, on the other side of the hump to do it all over again before everyone is let out, giddy, exhilarated and wobbly, while she rests and gets ready for another run with new riders. Once she got you in her clutches, you were trapped. There was nothing you could do. Just sit tight, endure, and enjoy.

For both me and Elaine that ride was ecstasy. We both knew that, unlike in our neighborhood, this wild and crazy monster with all her twists and turns and all her noise and bluster would eventually return us to safety. Back in The Bronx, on our street, all we could do was hope for the best, that we would make it home unmolested. Palisades Park was our fantasy.

That Saturday I had brought a lot of money with me. I spent most of it on that damn roller coaster. And the Wild Mouse, the Round-Up, the Ferris Wheel, bumper cars, flying saucers, and soggy, sour French fries. And at the end of the day, we took a ride in the Tunnel of Love.

We held hands, ate junk, walked the whole park many times, people watched, watched each other, went on the rides and oh yeah, most importantly, I won my girl a little black stuffed skunk. She called him Skunky. I got a kiss on the cheek for that. If you sank three regulation foul shots with a regulation basketball, you got to pick your prize. She picked out Skunky. Swish, swish, swish! Boy, was I lucky that day! I'm so happy my basketball higher power didn't let me embarrass myself. I couldn't have handled it if I had hit air balls. Thank you God!

Forty-five years later, I surprised Elaine with another little skunk. She told me what happened to the first one. After she got home from our date, Princess got hold of Skunky and disemboweled him.

We stayed until it got dark. They lit up some of those Hawaiian torches all over the park. We ate more French fries, went on the Cyclone one last time and then the three of us, me, Elaine and Skunky took the last bus home, holding hands, sleeping on each other's shoulders, never, ever, were we going to forget our big date that Saturday in July 1968.

Palisades has the rides,
Palisades has the fun.
Come on over.

I was debating whether to end the story here with this happy ending or tell you the truth. It's not that Palisades isn't true. It is. It all happened just like I said. It's just not where this story ends.

Towards the end of the summer Elaine got to meet the rest of my family. Everybody loved her. Me and Amy, mostly Amy, organized a party where Elaine could get a chance to meet everybody. It was great. We had potato chips, pretzels, and soda. The soul and salsa music was blaring. Amy got to dance with all my friends and me and Elaine danced slow, real slow. But I didn't try to kiss Elaine in front of her dad.

Elaine's dad, Pat, brought her over to my place around seven and of course chaperoned until midnight when the party ended. He sat at the dining room table with a six pack of Rheingold and a pack of Luckies while he kept an eye on his cherished princess. I put an ashtray out for him for those long ashes hanging off his cigarettes and gave him a bowl of pretzels.

My dad came home around eight, saw Pat sitting at the table and right away welcomed him, and grabbed one of Pat's Rheingolds and a Lucky Strike. Out of the corner of our eyes, me and Elaine watched our dads just sitting there drinking, smoking, laughing, and talking. On top of the music and dancing and how great it was for me and Elaine to be together having fun, just seeing our dads hanging out and talking and laughing made our night.

We lived on the fourth floor of 185 McClellan Street, but my bedroom window faced east onto Sheridan Avenue. As I was looking out a few days after the party,

I saw Louis on the street half a block down Sheridan towards 166th. He was standing in front of the entrance of P.S. 90 talking to Frankie and Robert. Seeing Louis talking to those creeps made me feel like maybe I was right when I attacked him. Maybe he is one of them. Maybe he too is out to get me.

Just then I heard Amy talking to someone out in our living room. I went out and saw Amy and Mariester, Louis's sister, sitting on the couch with books in front of them talking about algebra of all things. I always liked Mariester. She was closer to Amy's age, seventeen, maybe eighteen, pretty and was always polite. She had a heavy Spanish accent and whenever I saw her she greeted me with a warm *Hola! Como estas?* I used to show off my Spanish and reply *Muy bien gracias, y tu?* She would get a kick out of that and always complimented me on my Spanish. Amy looked up at me and told me that she was helping Mariester in her summer school algebra course so she could pass her Regents Exam and graduate. I said *hola* to Mariester, did all the Spanish cordialities and turned to my sister and said, "Ame, can we talk?" She said okay and came with me into my bedroom where I pointed out the window to Louis talking with Frankie and Robert. I asked, "What the fuck is going on? Here you are bailing out his sister and there they are planning on how they're gonna fuck me up."

Amy said, "No dummy, let me tell you what's goin' on. I was gonna tell you tonight when I saw you, so here it is. I made a deal with Louis. I helped Mariester a few times earlier this year with English and biology and it got her through. Today, Louis came to me and asked if I could help her with algebra 'cause that was all she needed to graduate. They don't have any parents and Louis takes care of her. Seeing as how I go to Bronx Science he thought I must be a genius. So, I said yeah on one condition: he gotta get those fuckin' morons," as she pointed out the window at Frankie and Robert, "off my brother's back. That's what he's doin' out there. Comprende?"

"Yeah, *comprendo*," I said. "*Gracias*, Ame."

"Did you ever apologize to him like I told you?"

"No," I said.

"Now's a good time. Go!"

I went. I got out to the stoop and waited for Louis to finish talking to Frankie and Robert. He saw me sitting there and sat down next to me. Before he said anything, I told him I was sorry for what I did. I said, "I had a real bad day and lost my cool and took it out on you. I got confused, I—" Louis jumped in and said, "Fuggedaboutit. I heard what happened to you. It makes sense, man. I'm sorry you're goin' through all this shit. If it makes you feel better, those scumbags won't be botherin' you no more. I took care of that."

I asked, "How?"

"No worries, I got their number. Just do yourself a favor and lay low with your girl. The streets are mean. You're in a bad situation bein' white around here. Someday, none of this shit's gonna matter. Someday, a guy like me could be president and a guy like you can walk down the street with your Puerto Rican girl and nobody will pay any attention to how you are different colors. That's not today, my man."

I listened real intently. I realized Louis was not only tough but real smart, too. I nodded as he talked and I had a new feeling about this guy. I liked him. After talking to Louis and seeing him in a new light, it was starting to get real clear to me that everything going on—all this hate and fighting, all this white and Puerto Rican drama, all this stuff about how you can't have a Puerto Rican girl if you're white—it took on a whole different perspective: people are people. Mostly good. Some not so good. I stopped being afraid. Louis helped me to stop being afraid. We got up, shook hands, and he went into the building.

Summer was ending and me and Elaine each had our fifteenth birthdays that first week of September. We celebrated by going to the Kent movie theater on 167th and saw a crazy movie called *Barbarella*. The Kent was one of those old vaudeville theaters that had those high domed ceilings and weird cement statues of angels and lions on the walls. It had a great big stage, four feet off the floor that even had the old heavy velvet curtain pulled way back. The air was musty and hot and the seats were sticky. Hardly anyone else was in the theater. It was dark. We ate greasy popcorn and held hands. Real tight. Even though

Jane Fonda looked really good with hardly any clothes on up on the big screen, I barely noticed. All I needed and wanted was sitting right next to me in a sticky seat in the dark, squeezing my hand in the Kent movie theater.

We were both feeling that end of summer, beginning of the school year anticipation and anxiety. We were the same age, but I had skipped a year. Elaine was heading to the tenth grade at Taft, the neighborhood school a few blocks away up on 170th, and I was going into the eleventh grade at DeWitt Clinton way up the Grand Concourse in the North Bronx. The reason I ended up at Clinton rather than Taft was because in the ninth grade back at 82, my gym teachers and my favorite teacher, Mr. Gordon, all pushed me to go to DeWitt Clinton, so I could continue to advance both athletically and academically.

Boys came from all over The Bronx because it was the only public high school left in The Bronx where you could still get a good education. If you worked hard. Amy's school, the famous Bronx High School of Science, was right next door.

Life got real busy as school started up. I was getting into my new routines, homework, my after-school job messengering downtown, my weekend job in the plumbing shop and now I had team practice twice a week. I hadn't planned on being on a team, but my gym teachers in 82 had contacted Coach Lipsky telling him that I'd be a good candidate for the physical fitness team. One day when I was in the cafeteria eating lunch that first or second week of school, Coach Lipsky came up to me and started talking about his Marine Corps physical fitness team started way back when Kennedy was president. He said I looked fit and strong and invited me to try out. I did. I made the cut. Push-ups, sit-ups, pull-ups, squat thrusts, running. I loved it. The following year I was a senior and I was voted co-captain of the team. We won the championship that year.

My teachers from 82 had warned me about Taft, where Elaine and most of the kids in my neighborhood went. They told me you could buy heroin in the boys bathroom, get knifed in the cafeteria, and never learn how to add fractions or write a coherent paragraph.

After school started, me and Elaine hardly saw each other. In addition to going to different schools and my busy schedule, Elaine's mom pulled the reins in more than ever. The only time Elaine was allowed to leave the apartment was for school. Muggings, killings, store robberies were rampant. My barber, George, whose shop was across the street from the front entryway of my building, was shot and robbed the first week of September. After *Barbarella*, I think me and Elaine saw each other maybe twice.

I wish it had turned out differently for us.

Elaine's parents had enough of the bad neighborhood. In the beginning of October they moved out. That same week junkies jumped and stabbed my old man. My life changed dramatically after the stabbing; I was carrying that much more weight on my shoulders, filling his shoes.

Too bad I never got to benefit too much from that talk Louis had had with Frankie and Robert. It was too little, too late. There was no need. Elaine was gone. She moved about twenty blocks away to a slightly better neighborhood. Twenty blocks in The Bronx could have been twenty miles or twenty light years for all practical purposes. We lost each other. In a way, I felt some relief. I always worried about her in our neighborhood as I worried about everyone I cared about.

I don't think we ever got a chance to kiss. I mean, really kiss. But we'd always have Palisades.

CHAPTER FIVE

THE AWAKENING

I wasn't quite awake, wasn't asleep either when I heard the yelling and screaming. I knew it was my dad. It was around midnight. I hopped off the top bunk and found myself half dressed with my Louisville Slugger in my hand, the same bat I played sandlot baseball with down the block in the vacant lot where they tore down a burnt out building earlier in the year.

I had started sleeping with my clothes on and my baseball bat under my mattress six months ago, about the time my dad lost Wolf in a poker game. Without Wolf sleeping on his shelf behind the plate glass window, the junkies started breaking into my dad's plumbing shop again. One night, one of them threw a steel garbage can through the plate glass window. They cleaned my dad out. All the brass pipe and fittings and the tools that were lying around, not in the lock-up freezer, were stolen.

After that break-in, my dad used to sit in a wooden chair in the dark, facing the plate glass window, halfway down the length of the shop, with a hunting rifle across his lap. He was waiting for the junkies to come back. One night I heard the gun go off. From that point on, I slept with my clothes on and my bat under my mattress.

I landed with both feet on the floor. I took a quick look at the lower bunk and saw that Richard was fast asleep. I grabbed my Knicks sweatshirt, threw on my Pro Keds, and ran through the apartment and out the door, bat in hand.

When I got out to the hallway, I took the stairs four at a time until I hit the dark lobby eight flights down. I made a sharp turn to the left at the bottom landing, headed towards the door to the courtyard. As soon as I turned, I skidded, slipped, and then fell hard on the terrazzo on what felt like keys, coins, and a sticky liquid. I couldn't tell for sure what it was. I made my way to the half opened courtyard door. The door was metal with a thick, opaque cracked glass window. The courtyard was dark with only the light of the streetlamp shining from Sheridan Avenue. I was moving real fast, almost sprinting, to where I thought I heard the screaming and hollering. I jumped down the couple of steps off the stoop and made a quick right and then, half a block down shot left onto McClellan Street. I looked down the hill past the P.S. 90 schoolyard, about two blocks away, and saw my old man, the only one on the street. He was moaning, staggering, tripping over himself, and swearing. As I got closer I realized it wasn't just because he was drunk as usual. He had blood all over him and he was holding a gaping knife wound in his gut.

"I chased 'em. I almost got 'em. They didn't get a fuckin, dime," he bellowed in a kind of laugh. He held his stomach, blood gushing out, as he stumbled up the hill. His overalls, shirt, and jacket were soaked with blood. He was panting all out of breath from chasing the junkies for blocks after they mugged him in our hallway. I remember his brown leather work boots, wet with red splotches all over them, dripping onto the sidewalk, leaving a trail of blood behind him.

I used my bat for support like a crutch as I put my dad's arm around my neck and shoulders. I walked him up the hill towards our building. With the help of the bat, I eased him and then me down onto the stoop. He sat there bleeding, moaning, and holding his gut. My dad kept saying, "I chased 'em. I almost got 'em. They didn't get a fuckin' dime."

My family and the neighbors had already gathered near the stoop by the time me and my dad got there. I heard someone yell out, "I'll go call the cops." Another one responded, "Don't matter, they don't come here anyways."

I sat there cradling my dad's head and neck as he lay on my lap bleeding, moaning, groaning, and cursing. My mom took in the whole scene but didn't seem alarmed.

Maybe she was holding it together for me and my siblings. She told my dad to sit up and put his head between his knees because he was fading in and out of consciousness. My sister and brother were dazed. Richard was squeaking his teeth and Amy was pulling out her hair.

The streetlamp overhead was glaring down on us. Blood was pooling around me, all over my sweatshirt and my new white Pro Keds and the bottom step of the stoop. My dad was sputtering and muttering and going in and out of consciousness. My eyes scanned the crowd of scared and concerned neighbors hovering around us. Silently I was pleading for someone to come up with some way to help us, to help me.

For an instant I thought about driving him to the emergency room myself. It flashed in my mind that those keys I had slipped on with all the blood and loose change in the hallway were my dad's keys. If I only knew where the van was. Truth is, the van may have been further away from us than the hospital was. Sometimes you had to park three, four, even five blocks away to get a legal spot or you'd be towed by morning because of the alternate side of the street parking for the street sweeper trucks.

All this was buzzing around in my brain while trying to figure out my next move. In that moment thinking about the van, the keys, and how to get to the hospital, I also remembered that the van most often took two people to drive it. It was a 1967 light-green Dodge Sportsman van, the kind with a flat front because the engine was inside in between the driver and the passenger which was really handy because quite often, especially in the winter or when it rained, you had to adjust the butterfly choke on the carburetor or dry out the distributor cap and wires in order to start her up. All you had to do was pop the engine compartment cover, fix the metal rod in place to hold it open, and sit there comfortably working on it. Sometimes I did that when my old man was driving because the gas mixture was either too lean or too rich and I was the only one able to fine tune it just right.

But that wasn't the problem I was worried about just then. The bigger problem was the transmission. Woody, the mechanic at the Dodge dealer on Jerome Avenue, a drinking buddy of my dad's, would call him when there was an exceptionally good deal available. Woody had known my dad was on the lookout for a van and told him about this one. It was a year old, and had that marvel of American automotive engineering, the famous 225 cubic-inch, Slant Six engine, Chrysler's claim to fame, along with a three-speed column shift manual transmission. That was the clincher. The transmission had steel shift rods that connected to the column shifter and traveled down through the floor and back along the chassis to the gearbox. These rods got all mangled and would jam up one out of four times between first and second gear, making it impossible to shift. That's why my old man had gotten it so cheap. He paid $600 for a nearly new van. But 25 percent of the time, someone had to get out, get underneath with a crowbar, and unjam the rods so my dad would be able to continue shifting. Otherwise my dad never got out of first gear. Unjamming the shift rods was my job.

Even though I had just turned fifteen, I had already been driving for a year. From the time I was fourteen I was not only the plumbing apprentice for my dad's business, but also his chauffeur for when he was drunk. He took my learner's permit and creatively changed my birthdate on it in case we ever got stopped. Even though I could drive the van, I wasn't about to go into our dark building, root around for bloody keys, try to find the van, hope that it starts, hope that it shifts, and on top of all that try to get my dad to the hospital and then find a legal place to park. That was just too much, considering everything else going on that night.

I had all I could to do to keep my dad sitting upright and keep it together for my family. Believe it or not, with all this blood and drama I felt no rage or outrage. I felt no blame or hate. I don't think I was worried or scared. I think at that moment the thing I was feeling was the rush of adrenaline that gave me the stamina to do what I had to do.

The one feeling I do remember is shame. Despite the fact that this wasn't a typical night where my old man came home loud and drunk and stammering and ill-be-haved, it was nonetheless a scene. I was ashamed to show the neighbors this aspect of my family. I tried desperately there and later in the emergency room to understand why I didn't feel anything other than shame. Shouldn't I be scared? Shouldn't I be vengeful? Shouldn't I be alarmed? I know I didn't read those or any emotions in my mom. She seemed almost blank. Maybe she was in shock. Or maybe as a Bronx emergency room nurse she had become numb to this kind of stuff. This was just another stabbing. Maybe the fifth or fifteenth or fiftieth that week for her. I don't know. But this was my dad, her husband bleeding out here on our stoop.

I felt like I was acting or maybe starring in a play or a movie. In my mind's eye I was watching this unfold as if it was happening to someone else. It was like I was separate from me. Separated from my feelings. I was center stage, right in the middle of the stoop. The big lights from the streetlamp were on us. Still holding the bat in one hand, with the other hand I was propping up my bleeding, almost dying dad. I was eerily calm. This tragedy was playing out and the audience was my neighbors. My family members were supporting actors and the lights were bright. I was the star of the show because no one stepped forward to help, to take the lead. So I did. Despite my dad's warm blood on my clothes, hair, and hands, I shivered from the chill in the air that October night with the awareness that it was up to me to take the lead.

Finally, an opportunity to move in to first place and take control. Control was never an option before. Just skewed chaos. It made sense for me to finally prove that I could do it all. It wasn't only about me needing to prove something; life itself was way out of control and this was my way, my only chance to reign it in. For all of us.

My new role kicked into gear right there on the stoop that night when I yelled out to the crowd gathered around us, "Can somebody help us get to the hospital?" A guy who I had never seen before stepped up and said, "I got a car, I'll be right back."

We dragged my dad, yelling, mumbling, bleeding, and cursing into the back of this nice man's gypsy cab. I had blood all over me and I was still clutching the bat, now blood-soaked and gooey. Morissania Hospital was just a few blocks away on 167th Street just west of the Grand Concourse. We were there in no time. My mom ran in as she knew the place from working there and in a few minutes she came back out with a couple of nurses with a gurney. We got my dad onto it and they wheeled him in. I was about to go back to the man in the gypsy cab to get my bat and thank him, but when I turned around, he was gone. I never saw him again.

It was a busy night at the Morrissania emergency room. A gunshot wound and an axe assault were ahead of us. The doctor came out and assured us we would be next, and to "just hold on." He didn't look like a doctor. He looked more like my cousin who was a few years older than me. I had my doubts that this young guy was going to be able to help us. I went over to the nurse's station

and asked if they had an older doctor with more experience. It was a crazy busy night, but the nurse on duty, in
a kind voice with a Spanish accent, took a moment and
told me, "Honey, you don't have to worry, Dr. Schwartz
may look young, but he has plenty of experience with
this kind of thing. He got back from Vietnam about a
year ago and has been able to patch up people in much
worse condition than your dad. Your dad will be fine."
My mom came out of the back area with her nurse uniform and cap on ready to assist Dr. Schwartz, but of
course he wouldn't let her.

We were in a dimly lit basement corridor, streaked
grey vinyl tiles on the cement floor, off-white smudged
cinderblock walls, the smell of betadine and bleach and
piss in the stale air. There was a bare lightbulb hanging
from a cord about a foot above my head. A fly was buzzing around.

Amy and Richard and my mom were huddled around
the side of my dad's gurney staring down on him, looking
lost. I was at the head of the gurney, my waist against the
pillow, looking straight down on my old man. He seemed
unconscious. We waited in that basement for hours.

What stands out in my mind more than anything
that night is when my dad looked up at me from his
gurney. There was an IV drip going into the back of
his hand. The white sheets on the gurney had dark red
blood spots. My dad's eyes suddenly snapped open and
he looked directly up into my eyes, just mine, focused,

clearer, sharper than what should be possible for a man in his condition, possibly fatally injured, drunk and sedated. He reached his hand up, the one with the IV, and grabbed my forearm, and pulled me down to his head. I leaned in and put my ear inches from his lips. In a little more than a whisper, he spoke clearly and coherently: "Steve, we're gonna get 'em. When I get outta here, we're gonna get 'em." Then he released his grip as he passed out. The sedatives they had given him when he first rolled in had finally kicked in.

As I was watching my old man lying there, a little voice in my head was screaming at me: *Why aren't you feeling anything? What's gonna happen if we ever do find 'em?*

Dr. Schwartz appeared with three nurses. He gave me a nod and a little smile and then wheeled my dad away.

After the stabbing, I got permission from my school to take the week or so off. Seeing as how it was Amy and not me who got into the Bronx High School of Science, my classes at DeWitt Clinton High School were not accelerated, so keeping up would be no problem.

I decided I would give my mom all my messenger job pay instead of the usual half. I stayed close to home. I visited my dad several times a day in the hospital. He was getting better and better and the silver lining, if you could call it that from this whole crazy time, was that my dad for the first time in my memory was sober for more than a couple of days. He wasn't drinking, couldn't drink. I saw the most genuine sides of him that I had always sensed were underneath it all. He was kind, he was humble, polite, interested in my life, everybody's life. He seemed grateful to be alive but also for the care, rest, and attention he was getting.

After ten days, my dad came home. While he was recuperating, he hung out on a plaid vinyl fold-up lawn chair right in front of the stoop for most of the day. He spent time talking to the neighbors, reading the paper, doing some work in the shop, and waiting for me to get home from school or work so we could talk. He asked how my life was, school and my job. He was friendly and attentive to Amy and my friends. He even started to act like a father to Richard. Once I even saw them sitting on the stoop, talking and smiling together. I noticed my dad and my mom were softer together. They talked and joked and, one time I actually saw them hugging. I was in a great place in my life. I felt important, loved, appreciated, proud, and happy to be Hy's son.

One day when my dad was out in front of the stoop in his lawn chair, me and Marcus, a kid who just moved up from North Carolina and lived across the street, were walking down Sheridan Avenue bouncing my basketball. Marcus's mom and dad liked me and were happy when I reached out to him when they first moved in. I was his first white friend. Marcus had told me back home in North Carolina white people were never friendly to Black people. Mr. White, Marcus's dad, and my dad were becoming friends.

My dad and Mr. White were at the stoop shooting the breeze when me and Marcus stopped to talk a little with them. We then continued walking down Sheridan Avenue. We were on our way to the Greek diner on the corner of 167th to get a couple of coffees for our dads and some sodas for us. A half a block away, a kid leaned his head out a window from the fourth floor and spat on us. Of course, it hit me right on top of my head. I kind of knew this kid, he was always looking for trouble. I got so pissed off I ran up to his apartment, banged on his door and when his mother answered, she started screaming at me in Spanish. I yelled and screamed and told her to warn her son to never do that again.

After yelling at the kid's mom, I came back down to the street and me and Marcus continued on our way to the diner. Marcus was noticeably jumpy and agitated. He said, "Gog, you shouldn't a done that." I told Marcus not to worry. We got the drinks and when I got back to my stoop, I started to tell my dad about the kid who had spit on me. As I was standing looking down at my dad sitting on his lawn chair, his eyes suddenly bulged. In a flash, he reached his arm up and grabbed my forearm hard and yanked me downward. I hit the sidewalk face first, scraping my forehead. I got a bloody nose and the wind knocked out of me. Just before I hit the cement, I felt air moving behind my head and I heard a swoosh in my ears. The spitter's father, a gangster and a dealer, had come out looking for me with his bat to let me know he didn't approve of the way that I complained to his wife about his son. This was the same guy who had sicced his Doberman on Wolf the year before. Protecting us both, Wolf snapped the dog's neck.

My father probably saved my life right then. Had my dad been his old self, probably halfcocked or wishing he was, he never would have been able to calm this guy down.

Yeah, it was a great couple of months. My dad was sober every day for a while after the stabbing. We got to experience what it meant to have him, the true him, home. Calm, loving, sane. Crazy as it sounds, I think that was the first and maybe only time I ever felt we had an intact family. I met my dad for the first time. The dad I want to remember.

I knew he was drinking when he pulled up to me in the van and he said, "Get in. We got work to do." His speech was slurred and his face was red. I was playing stickball and as usual felt embarrassed by his drunkenness. He said, "I told you, that night in the hospital we were gonna get 'em. I'm ready now. Get in." I averted my eyes from my friends and slid into the seat and said, "Okay."

It had been about six weeks of him not drinking, but underneath it all I knew sooner or later it was bound to end. Stricken with sadness and shame, I fell back into that old familiar gloomy place. In a way it was worse than before. I had had a taste of what it felt like to be appreciated, cared for by my sober dad. Maybe I even felt loved.

For weeks, we drove around in the van. All different neighborhoods, all different times. Some of those times, as much as I vowed never to be like my father, I wished I had been drunk too. Anything to get away from that nagging, relentless, aching fear I walked around with. I saw my old man peer into hallways, look in stores, scrutinize faces, stare into people's eyes on the street. I couldn't help but agonize over the nightmare of if and when we ever did find them. Thank God we never did.

Life was back to normal. I met my mom to walk her home when she worked the night shift at Morrissania. I defended my brother in the street and at school. When my sister came home late from school or being with friends, I met her at the D train on the Grand Concourse. I worked my two jobs: messengering downtown after school and, on Saturdays, cleaning up and organizing the plumbing shop. I gave half my money to my mom.

The dread was back. The drunkenness came back. The turmoil came back. But one thing changed. My mom was more present. She was tougher. She started taking more of an interest in our lives, me and Amy especially. She asked us about school and friends, tried to cook more. It was obvious she was trying to be a better mom. She became more protective of us kids and for once she started to stand up to my old man. When I wanted to take a Saturday off work to take Elaine on a date, my father whined, "If

Steve doesn't work, there won't be any grocery money." My mother responded, "Stop arguing. If we need the money, I'll work an extra shift." He backed off. My stronger mother was stepping up more and more. I remember her going all out and making a beautiful dinner so I could introduce Elaine to the family. She did the same thing for Amy and her sailor boyfriend, Mike. As wonderful as this new attentiveness was, me and Amy were skeptical. We were waiting for our real mom to return, the meek and submissive one who more or less gave up on us when we were younger. The whole stabbing thing woke her up.

One day my mom came home and said, "We're moving. I found a nice place in the North Bronx to rent, an apartment in a two-family." We knew my old man would have real trouble moving. He didn't do anything that required change too well. I was both encouraged and depressed. Sad to lose my street friends and encouraged that my mom was stepping up to the plate. I asked her, "Is it safer?" She said, "I'm not sure, but it's whiter."

It had taken all I had to make this neighborhood work for me, to walk on the same sidewalk, go to the same bodega, and check out the same girls, albeit not too closely or else I'd be called out for eyeballing. On the basketball court, I could call "next" and sometimes I got a game. I identified as non-white. This safer, whiter neighborhood worried me.

We moved that spring of 1969. I said goodbye to my friends, told them I'd still be around. After all, I worked for my dad and the shop was in the building. They said I was selling out and never talked to me again.

On moving day, when me, Amy, and Richard got home from school, the moving truck was already loaded up with all of our furniture, double parked and ready to go. My dad's van was on the sidewalk backed up in front of the stoop, packed with boxes and odds and ends. He was at the wheel and my mom was in the passenger seat on the other side of the engine. Me, Amy and Richard climbed in and sat on a makeshift bench seat behind the engine compartment.

I smelled the booze. My father's face was red as a boiling lobster, his tongue folded up and protruding halfway out his mouth, his eyes in a squint, he was hunched over, his hands gripping the steering wheel—the telltale signs he was drunk, enraged, and ready to pounce. I said to my mom and siblings, "He's drunk. Get out of the van. We're not driving with him." My mom agreed. We took the bus.

CHAPTER SIX

BRONX BOYS

August 26, 2001, Gilsum, New Hampshire

"Yo, Bernstein! I been doin' this for thirty years. I call you on *my* birthday every fuckin' year to remind *you* to wish *me* a happy birthday. And then about a week later, I call *you* again to wish *you* a happy birthday. Some things never change."

I'm listening to the answering machine, debating with myself if I'm up for a conversation with Joe after losing my sister Amy, my nineteen-year marriage, and my dog all in the space of a year. Sometimes it was tedious with Joe. Talking about the same things, the job, the family, how he's just got a few months left to retire and get off the force and go back to teaching high school biology, shit going on in New York, blah, blah, blah. I never fully understood why he bothered with me. If not for him, there would be no friendship.

I let him talk and let the machine record. I went about my business. Sure enough, ten days later, he called me again on my birthday.

"Yo, Bernstein! What the fuck? Pick up. Happy fuckin' birthday! Don't make me come up there Bernstein, pick up the fuckin' phone, I wanna hear your voice, make sure you're still breathin'. . . "

You'd think between his emergency service cop job in Harlem and his wife and two little boys, he'd be a little too busy to worry about my birthday.

I thought about me and Joe for a moment while the answering machine was recording. I had known Joe for thirty-one years. I met him in 1970 doing push-ups. We were both fifteen.

* * *

When I got to Allerton Avenue, the "white" neighborhood where my mother moved us after my dad got stabbed, I wasn't sure what to expect. In the old neighborhood on Sheridan Avenue in the South Bronx, I was the only white kid, yet I dared to have a Puerto Rican girlfriend and I never ever backed down from a fight. Sure, I felt alienated at times, but I also felt at home. I felt at home with people of color. I felt at home with gangs. I felt at home hanging out on the stoop. I had soul and salsa and basketball in my blood. In the white neighborhood, I had none of that. And no real stoops.

The people on the street were white. There were Italian bakeries and Jewish delicatessens. There was a Greek diner. The kids in the parks and schoolyards were white. They were mostly playing baseball, stickball, and football. I didn't have to call "next" for a basketball game, like in my old neighborhood, never being sure if I'd ever get a game. Not here. Not in this neighborhood. Nobody was playing basketball. I had the courts to myself.

It was safer for my mother and brother on the street. The new neighborhood didn't matter much to my dad. He was in his own drunken world and hardly around as usual. Parking the van was easier. We had a driveway.

Richard was now going to a decent junior high school where he wasn't tormented as much as in the old neighborhood. In his old school, he was teased and beaten up. His bus pass and lunch were often stolen from him. On the days that I was able to get out of school early enough, I would meet him after his school ended and fend off any bullies to make sure he got home safely. In the new neighborhood he got home safely on his own.

Amy got married right after high school. At least she was out of the house now. When she came for a visit, shit would happen. My old man would pick on her and tease Ben, her new husband. At least she had the luxury of physically leaving. I'm glad she had that escape.

I visited Amy and Ben at least once a week. We ate TV dinners on folding tray tables. It was fun. She was doing pretty good, working in an office and going to City

College, and being married. I was happy for her. Amy got out from under my dad's insanity. She tried to find sanity in her new life. She had bouts with eating disorders and the old hair pulling behavior. She went to therapy. She tried to help Richard as much as possible.

My world got a little boring, relatively speaking. No fights. Nobody out to kill me. Sadly, no Elaine. Just school, practice with the high school physical fitness team, work and work. I still went back to the old neighborhood because the plumbing shop was there. I worked there one afternoon during the week and all day Saturday.

After school, two days a week, I worked out with my team. In our makeshift unventilated training room at DeWitt Clinton, a former storage room, we trained hard: super sets of push-ups, sit-ups, pull-ups, and squat thrusts. If the indoor track wasn't being used, we practiced running drills. The hallway was for broad jumping and the stairwells for aerobic endurance. If it wasn't raining or snowing, we ran 2.2 miles around the Jerome Park Reservoir.

To my surprise, I missed my gang. I longed for my street life that had been such a big part of my world in my old neighborhood. I craved that feeling I had with Elaine. It's crazy, but even with all the drama I experienced in the South Bronx, I felt the loss of it. I was aching for basketball, a bodega, blaring soul music, and a stoop. A real stoop.

The buildings in the new neighborhood were smaller single or attached homes and a few apartment buildings.

Sure, these buildings may have had a few stairs out front, but they weren't a real stoop.

How you know it's a real stoop is not so much what it looks like, but rather what happens on it. A stoop is a place to socialize. People hanging out, reading the paper, playing dominos or cards, talking and gossiping, smoking, eating a hero with the waxed paper laid on their lap, playing congas, shooting craps, listening to the radio, rocking babies to sleep, playing with the dog, braiding hair, drinking coffee, soda or beer, and later in the evening, kissing and sometimes a little bit more. People would bring out milk crates to sit on, folding chairs, card tables, and battery operated portable record players. And, if the Yankees were playing, the TV would come out too, attached by a series of extension cords threaded through a window. Stoop sitting included the mothers and grandmothers who sat in a front window, a pillow on the window ledge under their elbows, as they kept a close eye on the children playing in the street.

I never saw anybody on the so-called stoops in the new neighborhood. My white neighbors were more private. They preferred to socialize in their kitchens and living rooms or behind the house, in their tiny cement backyards, enclosed by cinderblock or brick walls.

The neighborhood was clean, with mostly well-kept little brick houses. There was kind of an old country Italian feel to it. Older ladies with black shawls walking to the grocery store with their fold-up shopping carts and

people talking Italian on the street. Vito's, the little corner store, was this neighborhood's version of a bodega.

Coach Lipsky awarded me my white satin DeWitt
Clinton jacket with a big black embroidered C and the
JFK presidential insignia for outstanding fitness merit.
As a junior I felt proud to wear it because most often
letter jackets were awarded to seniors. I wore that jacket
all the time. I made sure to wear it on the streets of the
new neighborhood like a badge of honor, to distinguish
me from everyone else in the hopes of sending out the
message: Do not mess with me.

Columbus High School was a few blocks away from
my new apartment. Sometime in the spring Clinton and
Columbus had a fitness team competition. Both teams
were vying for the city championship. Clinton, being
the current city champ, held home-court advantage. So
Columbus came to Clinton and the two teams squared
off. The Clinton team consisted of twelve kids. All of us
were various body types and sizes but all fit and strong
and ready to defend our championship against anybody.
There were nine Puerto Ricans, two Black kids, and me
on the team. Columbus, of course, was all white. The
coaches knew each other well and were quite friendly.

Columbus got set up in the gym and was warming up
when my team made its entrance. We came into the gym,
took off our satin Clinton jackets and folded them up
neatly and placed them on the bleachers. Without hesi-
tation or discussion, we immediately formed a line and

got into the push-up position. We stayed lined up like that, waiting for Columbus to follow suit. The two teams lined up head to head in the plank position, waiting for the whistle.

The first event of six was push-ups. The minimum you were allowed to do to compete was sixty in a minute. You go for two minutes. The record at the time was 125 in two minutes. Our graduating captain held that national record. The push-ups had to be perfect. That meant back straight, locked elbows on the up, and chest tapping the mat on the down. Eyes forward.

While we were waiting for the whistle, the Columbus guy who was head to head with me started talking to me. That never happened. Clinton was always focused, serious, never gave the competition a friendly or an unfriendly gesture. Until of course after the competition, when Clinton always won.

The Columbus kid said, "You're the new guy on the block. I recognized the jacket. My name is Joe."

I replied, "Steve."

Joe did 119 push-ups and I did 120 that day. After the meet, Joe came up to me and congratulated me on Clinton's win. He told me he lived on Allerton Avenue, down the block from my apartment. I invited him to come over to my place on Sunday to lift weights in my garage.

From that moment on, Joe and I were friends for life. From what I could tell, he came from a pretty functional and loving family, if there is such a thing. He had a twin brother, Nicky, who was on the wild side. He was into a lot of pot and played in a band. Joe was different. He was ultra-responsible, hardly drank, and took care of his parents. His dad, Joe Sr., was on the older side for being the parent of someone Joe's age. He was pushing sixty when I met him. Joe Sr. was an upholsterer and talked with a thick Italian accent. Joe's mother, Mary, was funny and pretty. She was one of those Irish women who on the outside seemed very Catholic. But when she got to know you those mischievous twinkling eyes and her wry and irreverent sense of humor dispelled any illusion of her being a religious goody two shoes. She talked about her childhood with her sister, now Sister Margaret, a nun, and the fun they used to have growing up in Hell's Kitchen.

I remember the time Mary invited me over for dinner. I got to meet Spider, their little dachshund dog, and Mary's sister, Sister Margaret, was there too. I anticipated some kind of Italian feast like lasagna or spaghetti and meatballs, seeing how Joe is half Italian and his old man has the accent and everything, and how Joe is always cursing in Italian but that was not to be. We had tuna sandwiches. Mary, if I remember right, was not big into cooking. Dinner was great. Joe's dad asked me about my family and my plumbing apprenticeship. He thought it was great that I knew a trade. Sister Margaret was very short and she had a big cross on a rosary bead necklace around her neck with the whole nun habit and hat on.

She told a few corny jokes. I thought she was nice and normal considering she was the first nun I ever met. By the time dinner was done, Margaret pointed to the silver ring on her ring finger and said she had to get back to her husband and it was nice meeting me. Even me, the Jewish kid, knew that nuns don't marry so in a perplexed manner I looked over at Joe and then Mary. They all started laughing and pointed up to the ceiling, indicating Sister Margaret is married to God. I thought for a moment and laughed too.

There were plenty of girls in the neighborhood. They were all dolled up and made up and poofed up like they were always going to a party. They mostly congregated together, all dressed up with nowhere to go. The guys had slicked-back hair, a cigarette behind their ears, and a Bronx accent that made me sound cultured and sophisticated. If my old neighborhood was *West Side Story*, this one was *Grease*.

Joe's friends were mostly Italian and Irish and heavy into drinking and drugs. Joe was different. Joe was an athlete. He was clean. He would have a few gulps of the Boone's Farm apple or strawberry when the bottle came around. I never saw him take a hit of pot.

He grew up with this crowd and didn't want to make too many waves. The racism was so thick you can cut it with a knife. If there were people of color around, they would have been cut with a knife. Niggers this. Spics that. All day long. I wondered how Joe's friends would have made it in the South Bronx. They can be prejudiced all they want up here, everybody's white! All these guys would have been dead if they actually talked that way around people of color.

I stayed clear of all of them. Joe sought me out all the time. Out of habit, he carried around the same racist MO as his goombahs did. But it was just a show, I suspected. He knew better than to talk like that around me. I told him off a few times. As soon as he started in with the nigger and spic shit, I would say, "Joe, shut the fuck up. You wanna hang with me, you gotta stop that shit." He was always so pliable, so subject to peer pressure. He would change back in a second when he was with his buddies. After a while he admitted he didn't really feel that way and thanked me for helping him be the man he wanted to be.

One day I was sitting on Joe's stoop, shooting the shit with him and his brother, Nicky. It wasn't really a stoop, just a set of stairs leading to a private house connected to eight other private houses, each with their own set of stairs in front of them. The steps weren't stone or granite like on a real stoop. So, they were stairs not stoops and they were houses not buildings, so technically, we were sitting on the stairs.

Joe's friends saw us there and started coming over. They were drinking beer out of cans in little brown paper bags, but they were definitely fucked up on more than beer that day. Joe gave Nicky a nudge with his elbow and said, "Uh oh. We got company." Nicky and Joe tensed up because their parents didn't want these guys drinking in front of their house.

As usual, Joe didn't say anything to his friends about the drinking in front of his house. As usual, I didn't want to hang around these guys and got up to leave just as a woman was walking by the house. One of Joe's drunk friends took his beer can out of the paper bag and threw it at her as he yelled, "We don't want any niggers here!" I knew the woman was a caretaker because she wore a uniform similar to a nurse and I had seen her pushing an elderly person in a wheelchair one time.

Joe instinctively grabbed my arm. I glared at him. I shook off his hold on my arm and ran over to the woman who just as soon wanted to avoid the whole thing. After picking up the can I apologized to her. I dropped the can in the trash, looked back at Joe and his friends, and went home, sad and furious. When is all this racial shit going to end?

The woman in the nurse's uniform reminded me of all the times I had protected my mother as she walked home from her night shift as an emergency room nurse in my old neighborhood. Crime was colorblind. Anyone was a target. If the junkies saw you and wanted to mug you, they would, no matter what color you were. But the junkies were a minority and I never saw any of my neighbors sitting on their stoop yell out a racial slur or throw something at a passerby. The stoop was the place to mingle.

Here, in the middle of the day, a fucked-up, drunken white kid could sit on the front steps of a house and throw a beer can at a woman of color and yell racial slurs. This hatred was worse than anything I had experienced as a minority in my old neighborhood. This hateful attitude by white people reminded me of the bigotry of the white kids on the basketball court in Delaware when I visited Isaac. Same hatred, same skin color, different accents.

Joe's friends were white and so was I, but there was no way I was ever going to be like them. Even though we were all the same color, I was still different. South Bronx, North Bronx, I was always different, always an outsider.

I learned right way if you were renters like us, you were considered second class. Every time one of Joe's friends asked where I lived, and I would say we were renting the downstairs of the D'Allesio's house, they'd say, "Whatsamatta? Can't afford your own house? I thought Jews were rich."

One day I parked my old man's car a few houses down from our place in the only vacant spot on the street. A guy came storming out from his house and screamed at me. He told me I had parked in his spot and had to move it. I said, "You kiddin'? Where's it say this is your spot?" He said, "You wanna spot? Buy a fuckin' house like the rest of us," as he pulled aside his shirt and exposed a small pistol stuck into his waistband. I moved the car around the corner. This neighborhood was right out of *The Sopranos*.

School was my salvation. Granted, there were no girls there, but I grew to realize there was a benefit to not having that distraction. I did great in academics, I had my fabulous team, and I worked. Clinton wasn't immune to racial tension. There were a few race riots—buses turned over and fighting out in the street—but for the most part, if you went there, you had to keep your nose clean. The eight thousand boys passed up their local high schools and came from all different Bronx neighborhoods because they wanted to be at Clinton. If you screwed up too bad, the administration would ship you back to your local high school.

Wearing that Clinton jacket in my new neighborhood was a clear message that I was different. In that jacket, I was king of the mountain, or at least that's how I felt, how I needed to feel. I went to the tough school, the all-boys famous school. Clinton had the best teams. Clinton produced the most college-bound students. As much as that jacket symbolized my differentness, it also gave me street credibility.

In the South Bronx I had stood out; I was different because I was white and I paid a price for that difference. Here, we are all white. I'm white and they're white so I had to find a way to distinguish myself. My white Clinton jacket helped to establish my distinct identity; I was different and, in my mind at least, I was better than them.

Turned out Joe was different, too. He wanted a change and welcomed my difference. He recognized that I offered a more compassionate model of toughness than his neighborhood buddies.

I remember going to Joe's house a lot. His mother was so kind and loving. Me and Joe were going out one night to the White Castle hamburger joint over on Boston Road. I remember vividly, because it struck me so deeply when Mary, his mother, reached into her purse and said, "Here, take this couple of bucks, Joey. Go out and have a good time with your friend. Here, take this, go."

I know it's a big nothing. A mother should give her kid money to go have fun with a friend. But when Mary said, "Here, Joey, go have fun, take this," I thought, *that* was a mother. Of course I always had money—I earned it. I got this pang, this jolt in my gut and chest whenever she said, "Joey, here take this. Go have fun," with two or three dollars in her hand. At that moment I wanted her for a mother.

The White Castle, now that was something. Three bucks! That was enough for about a dozen hamburgers, a thick shake, and some french fries. I say hamburgers and thick shake loosely. The fries were more like strings. The burgers, for lack of a better word, were about the size of a half dollar. Not just the diameter but also the thickness. You could walk out with a whole bag of these burgers, with the relish, onion, and ketchup and the little rolls and, in less than two bites each, make a meal of it. In our book that was living large.

Those late White Castle nights, a second dinner for both of us, were the times me and Joe talked. Eating out of our greasy White Castle paper bags we walked and talked. I told him about my life. He told me he was sick of the kids in the neighborhood. He told me how it's almost like he has to put on an act to be like them. Like them, meaning acting like little Mafiosos—like they owned the world, and girls and Blacks and Puerto Ricans were shit. Joe was not like that. He said that's why he liked hanging out with me. He knew I was tough. He knew I was pretty much emancipated from my parents. I acted like an adult. He wanted to be like me. I didn't have to tell him about my situation with my dad. He saw it all. My old man came home drunk a few times, embarrassed me on the street by cursing and calling me and anyone I was with names, threatening nonsense. During our White Castle binges, he offered his basement to me if I needed a place to stay. He said his parents liked me but they worried about me. He said his mother was happy that I was a good friend for "her Joey."

That's pretty much how the rest of the school year went. School, work, team practice, me and Joe working out shooting the shit. I worked all that summer with my dad. In September, my senior year, I turned sixteen. I was now legally driving with a legitimate driver's permit.

My old man let me use his '66 Dodge 440 Coronet. It was baby blue and looked like a family car, but I'll tell you what, it was a beast. Same chassis and drive train as the Charger, just dressed down and more conservative. Great car. Fast. It had a 318 cubic-inch V-8. Best engine

Detroit ever made. Unfortunately, it had a leaky rear seal and every fifty miles or so the engine would seize. The car would stop dead. All you had to do was coast to the curb and "park" as straight as you can. Next, put a couple of quarts of motor oil in the crankcase and she'd start right up again. I used to stock up and buy three cases of oil at a time. It was cheaper that way. To my dad's credit, he said, "You keep that thing in gas and oil and I'll let you drive it once in a while."

Joe liked having a best buddy with wheels. It made him feel important. Not only was he the only one out of his buddies who had access to wheels, I even taught him how to drive it. The first time the Coronet stalled out with Joe at the wheel, he let go of the wheel, yelled "*Va fongool*," jumped out of the car, and kicked the tire. "Why'd it stop like that?" he asked. "I didn't step on the brake." I got my Italian curse word lessons with Joe, mostly courtesy of the Coronet.

One afternoon after Joe's football practice we were on our way to my house to work out in my garage and we came to a stop sign on Allerton and Hone. Stopped just ahead of us was a big old dump truck loaded high with landscaping tools and brush. Suddenly, the truck starts backing up, not seeing us. I honked and threw it into reverse but it was too late. He crashed right into the front end of the Coronet. This big, round, unshaven, gruff guy chewing a Di Nobili cigar jumps out of the cab with a bat in his hand and starts yelling at me. Joe told me those skinny cigars were called "guinea stinkers" because they smelled so foul. Anyway, he walked towards the car, gesticulating in Italian. He was ready to kill me. Joe knew of this guy and told me he was known as Guido. Joe said, "Steve, you better let this slide." Obviously I didn't get Guido's insurance information. Probably didn't have any.

After the crash, every time I came to a stop, the hood flew open. Joe gave me a big, thick rope his dad had in the garage so I could tie the hood down. My old man was furious and told me I better figure out a way to get the hood and bumper fixed.

If that wasn't bad enough, Joe, who by this point felt like part owner of the Coronet, insisted on putting a local politician's bumper sticker on an undamaged part of the bumper. I hardly noticed it but evidently Sal Labolida, a politician up on Gun Hill Road, was a gangster who Italians loved and Blacks hated. The first day I brought the car to Clinton, the windshield got smashed. A school buddy of mine told me some of the Black guys in school didn't appreciate the bumper sticker.

So now the Coronet had a twisted bumper, a scrunched and popping open hood semi-secured with a rope, a smashed windshield, and, of course, every fifty miles or so, the engine seized. My old man gave me the car.

The father of one of Joe's friend's owned a junkyard and found me a windshield for twenty-five bucks that he guaranteed would fit. One afternoon me and Joe smashed out the old windshield and did our best to put the new one in the opening. Come to find out the "guaranteed to fit" windshield was from a '67 Plymouth Fury which was slightly different than the '66 Dodge Coronet. From then on I had to drive very carefully and make sure the oil was always topped off or the engine would suddenly seize, the car would stop short, the hood could pop open, and the windshield could fly off.

As spring of my senior year approached, me and Joe were in full swing with our training sessions. We trained for our respective teams almost every day. We competed fiercely, all in good spirits in the service of becoming better athletes for our teams. This also gave definition to our new friendship.

I had my sights set on beating a record before I graduated. Joe made sure I kept on task by helping me train. I was going for the national high school sit-up record. I had to beat 3,500 in I forget how much time. Joe pushed me to do five hundred sit-ups in one session, along with three sets of ten with a hundred-pound barbell behind my neck. Every day. I broke the record with five hundred to spare. Four thousand sit-ups! Couldn't have done it without Joe's help. That's the kind of friend he was.

Joe knew I loved basketball, and one day he came up with an idea. He said, "Hey, Bernstein, instead of going down five blocks to the Columbus schoolyard and not have anybody to play with, why don't we build a basketball court right here on our street? Probably, nobody will play with you here either, but if you teach me, I'll play."

Joe ran into Vito's and came out with a basketball rim. He said Vito gave it to him if he would stock shelves for a week. As Joe pointed to the telephone pole, he said Vito made clear we could put it up right there as long as we didn't break his window.

Joe pulled this whole idea together as a present for me. As I was looking up at the telephone pole, I took the rim from Joe and said, "Thanks, man." It really was a good spot. Next to no traffic and right next to Vito's if we got thirsty and wanted a Coke. Joe said his old man had a ladder and I said my old man had a piece of plywood. In fifteen minutes, we were each back, me with the plywood, hardware, and tools and Joe with the ladder.

I knew that the hoop needed to be ten feet off the ground so I took out my folding ruler and was careful to accurately measure along the pole and mark it with a yellow carpenter's crayon. I made sure to measure from the street and not from the sidewalk which would have made the hoop six inches too high. Joe thought I was a genius. He said, "Wow, Bernstein, you know your shit!" Within an hour, we had ourselves a court. I got my dusty and deflated basketball out and pumped it up with my bike pump. Joe learned how to dribble that day. Sort of.

In a matter of days, that hoop on that telephone pole on that corner of Allerton and Lurting became the social hub of the neighborhood. All of Joe's friends and a few guys we didn't know, but got to know better, showed up and wanted to play ball after seeing me and Joe having so much fun. I told them the rules including the rule that there would be absolutely no racial slurs or any kind of violence or they would be kicked off the court. Everybody followed the rules.

A few guys knew the game, the rest were awkward and couldn't ever get the hang of it. Including Joe. It didn't matter. I was happy for once to be a star. I got "ooohs" and "aaahs" with every jump shot I made, which was just about all of them. For the ones that clanked off, I would hear a collective "awww." It was fun being king of the court. A benefit of this white neighborhood.

The girls started to show up, too. They stood along the curb like cheerleaders, giggling and pointing. Most nights, I would "shoot the lights out" and get the "ooohs" and "aaahs" from all the girls chewing and popping gum, with the mascara and hair-sprayed hair and long red nails and skintight pants and padded bras. These skinny Barbie dolls really didn't do much for me. They seemed fake. I missed Elaine and those feelings I had.

I missed real ballplayers. And as much as being a superstar on the corner of Lurting and Allerton up in the North Bronx was great, I still felt alone. These were Joe's people, not mine. Never mine.

Then, after the game I would go down my block and they would go down theirs. Sometimes Joe would go with me and sometimes he would go with them and that was life.

On balance, life was better in this neighborhood. It was the most peaceful time of my teen years because I wasn't fighting for my or my family's safety like in the old neighborhood.

At home, I took less of my old man's shit. Mainly because he wasn't home that much. Part of my mom's stepping up to the plate, like moving us to this neighborhood, was telling my dad not to come home drunk. She told him to stay in the shop. And for the most part he listened.

Amy wasn't around to be victimized by him anymore. Richard was safer. My mother was safer.

I only had half days the last month of school. My Regents exams were completed. If you had good grades, they let seniors off early. So, I worked with my old man more. Driving him, working jobs, just about running the business. It got so that my old man couldn't run the business too well without me.

I started devising a plan. My exit plan. Why not? The family wasn't in crisis. I was not abandoning a sinking ship, like it would have been had I run away at fifteen when my old man got stabbed and my whole family was in peril in the old neighborhood. Life was better now. Maybe this was *my* time to get out, get away while the getting was good. I had my diploma, my construction skills, quite a bit of cash saved up, and now it was time for me. So, I started to plan my trip. My bicycle trip.

I was going to go from The Bronx to Canada on my ten-speed classic Schwinn Continental with the chrome fork. And never return. I told my family that it was time that our extended family started healing old wounds and start talking again. I was going to go to Montreal to visit my favorite aunt, my mother's younger sister, Aunt Bea. My plan was to break the ice and end a six-year estrangement during which my mother's siblings had banished her from the family following the death of Grampa.

That's what I told my family. My real plan was to run away, ride away, and not come back.

As high school was winding down and I was transitioning to full-time work with my old man, I started to put my itinerary together. Amy and Ben had bought some bikes and went on a small trip to Long Island. They took the Long Island Railroad and then had a trip laid out where they would see the sights by bike and hit many of the beaches. Amy told me about something very cool: the AYH, the American Youth Hostels. She told me for cheap money you could stay in places all over the country while you were either biking, hiking, skiing, or horseback riding. You could have a car under special circumstances. This AYH thing was perfect. I could live cheap on the way to Canada, cook my own meals, maybe meet some interesting people on my trip and not have to worry about where to stay for a while. I took the train downtown, found the AYH office, and bought a $20 membership and got my own AYH card.

After laying out the route from The Bronx all the way up to Montreal via youth hostels, it turned out to be somewhere around four hundred miles. Some of the hostels were as much as sixty miles apart from each other. I needed to get into good bike shape for rides like that.

I went down to Eddie's bike shop where I had originally bought my two Schwinns. The first one was the five-speed Collegiate when I was twelve with my kosher meat market money. It was stolen less than a year later right out from under me. A gang of Puerto Rican kids came up to me while I was giving my brother a ride on the handlebars. They surrounded us and one of them said, "Your brother or your bike."

When I was thirteen, me and Isaac got our ten-speed Continentals, with the chrome fork. Several steps up from the five-speed Collegiate, no chrome fork. I was able to afford this luxury vehicle with my savings which were a combination of bar mitzvah money, Saturday clean-out-the-shop money, and basketball hustle money.

Once I told Eddie about how my Collegiate was stolen, he gave me a real good price on all the gear I needed for the trip. I got one of those German aluminum rat traps, a pair of big and strong, black canvas saddle bags, a bunch of bungee cords, two canteens, extra inner tubes, patch kits, tire tools, a dog bone wrench with all the nut sizes, a fold-up tool kit, a pump, extra brake shoes and hardware, a clip-on head lamp, waterproof matches, waterproof cases for my maps, a mess kit, and a bunch of other gear I can't recall. Eddie even gave my bike a free tune-up and taught me how to do one on the road, just in case. He flipped the bike upside down on its seat and handlebars and showed me the best way to adjust the brakes and the gears. Doing it my way for the last two years frayed the cables. He put new ones on. No charge for the lesson or the cable.

Early every morning, two hours before school started, I rode my bike to Clinton. I put forty pounds of barbell weights in the saddlebags and strapped a few on top of the rat trap, too. My school was only three miles away so the ride gave me a little bit of a workout, but not much. But I did get a workout carrying my bike with all the weights up and down two flights of stairs just as the other boys were arriving to school. I wouldn't have left my bike outside even if there had been bike racks. The only safe place in the school building for my Continental was locked up inside the physical fitness room.

As I rode home from Clinton one afternoon, I saw Joe walking home from Columbus. He took one look at me and my bike and asked, "Bernstein, what the fuck you doin' with your bike loaded up with weights like that?" That's when I told him about my plan. Not the running away part. Just the bike trip, the hostels, my aunt, the Canada part. I saw him taking it all in and then he said, "What the fuck, Bernstein? You weren't gonna invite me?"

I hesitated a minute, as I had planned on going solo but I changed my mind and said, "Joe, waddya think? Sure I was. I just needed to get my bike and me in shape and then I was gonna tell you all about it."

He said, "Fuckin' beautiful! Give me a half hour. Let's meet up at your garage early and we'll talk about it before we lift at four."

As I was riding home I had a long conversation with myself. I didn't want to tell him the truth. That I was running away. He'd try to talk me out of it. But on the other hand, wouldn't it be nice to have my buddy with me? And then I thought, wait a second, I never saw Joe even ride a bike. Does he even have one?

When we started our workout that afternoon, Joe came right in and said, "I'm goin' with you." I asked what kind of bike he had. He didn't have one. Then I asked, did he ever have a bike? "Nope." So, then I had to ask, "Do you know how to ride a bike?"

He said, "What the fuck? What do you take me for?"

"No disrespect, Joe. It's just I never saw you with a bike. You never talked about a bike, that's all."

He said, "I rode my cousin's bike when we were younger."

"Your cousin live around here?" I asked.

"Used to," he said.

"Okay," I said. "So, when did he move?"

"About ten years ago."

"So the last time you rode a bike was what? When you were six?"

"Yeah, I guess so."

"So, did you have training wheels or what?" I kidded.

"Fuck you," he said and he threw his sweatband at me. Then he added, "I have a plan." Joe told me how

179

he wanted me to sweet talk his mother into giving him permission and money to go on the trip and to get a bike and all the gear.

I looked at him and said, "You're fuckin' nuts!"

For the next half hour, he told me how I was going to do it. He said his mother likes to have a cup of tea and a biscotti at Sal and Dom's Bakery.

Joe had already told Mary that I had an idea that I wanted to "run by" her so she knew as soon as I asked her out for a cup of tea that I was playing her. Mary knew that the best way to get intel about Joe was to pump Nicky for information. As twins, they told each other everything. Joe told Nicky that I was going up to Canada on a bike trip and I was going to meet all kinds of girls along the way. Evidently Nicky had told Mary about the trip so she already knew what I was up to.

Mary and I sat at a tiny table at Sal and Dom's bustling bakery on Allerton Avenue, surrounded by tall, bright white fake wedding cakes with plastic brides and grooms perched on top and chilled display cases full of cannoli and other powdery and gooey white pastries that I had no clue what they were. Mary had her tea and biscotti and, to show my sophistication, I ordered an espresso with a twist of lemon peel, just like my dad always ordered at the mafia joints on Arthur Avenue.

Mary did all the talking. First off, she said, "I love my Joey more than life itself." She said he was the quiet one of the two twins. Never had any trouble, was always a

good boy, looked out for his parents, and kept his nose
clean. She told me that Joey never really fit in with the
neighborhood idiots. "He was always more kind and
thoughtful than the drunken bums around here. They're
just like their parents," she said. She told me he's been
growing up a lot lately. He seems nicer, more thoughtful.
He hangs around with these bum friends of his less and
less. "It's because of you," she said. I looked at her and
felt for a second like she was blaming me for something.
Then I realized what she said was a good thing. "Then
you show up," she said. "A Jewish kid, no less, from the
South Bronx, who's smart, nice, has a job, got out of high
school, what, two years early? No drugs, no drinking,
doesn't take any shit from anybody and plays basketball
like a Black kid. Somehow you know things, somehow
you're so much older than your age. I know your sister
left at eighteen, that your old man's a drunk, that hardly
nobody sees your mother, and that your brother got
problems. Joey tells me everything and he thinks you're
the greatest. I don't get it. Jews don't act like you. They
don't go into trades, they don't get drunk like your dad,
they can afford their own place. It don't add up.

"Truth is, first time you came to the house, you saw
my husband lugging his tool bag into the cellar and
asked him if he needed help. The hooligans around here
never did that, their whole lives! And then you rescued
the DeCurtis's little dog. He coulda got squished on
Allerton, Joey told me. Not that it would mean anything

to you, but Moira, Joey's friend forever, next door, told me how all the girls are always checkin' you out around here and you don't give any of 'em the time of day. Joey tells me you hardly ever get upset, you keep your cool. That's good." She looked off to the side like she was thinking about something, figuring it out and then said, "You're not really sixteen, that's just how long you been breathin'." She finished our one-way chat with: "I like you, I trust you. Take Joey on this trip with you. Please, please, look out for my Joey." She reached out her hand and as I took it into mine, I saw tears in her eyes. She said, "He has to go on this trip with you, he needs to. It'll be good for him."

The next day Joe came down to my garage. Willie, the landlord, was mowing the lawn, a ten by ten patch of grass on the side of the house. Sometimes you could see Willie working his pigeons up on the roof. He knew Joe from the neighborhood. As Joe was passing by, with a smirk he called out to Willie, "Hey, Mr. D'Allesio, how ya doin? How are them homing pigeons of yours? You lose any lately?" Willie laughed, waved, and kept mowing. When Joe came in to start lifting, I asked him about Willie. He told me about how Willie's fancy daughter and son-in-law used to live in my apartment and shared the house with Willie and his wife, Olympia.

Joe told me that Willie's daughter's husband was a loan shark and came into a lot of money and moved to New Jersey. That's how the apartment came up for rent.

I understood more now. My apartment was nice, but it was also showy. It had wallpaper with felt designs and plush blue carpeting in the living room which was up three stairs from the rest of the apartment. The living room was off limits. I think the rental agreement said no kids or animals allowed in the living room. I think I was in there once or twice the whole time I lived there.

I asked Joe what the deal was with the pigeons. He told me a lot of older Italian guys have them. They keep them in coops on the roof and race them. He told me one time, one of Willie's birds got a little lost and landed at Joe's house. That's how they got to know each other. One day Joe saw his dog Spider trying to play with this pigeon in the backyard. The bird kept flapping her wings, driving Spider crazy. Joe told me from his patio, you can see Willie on the roof working the birds. That's how he knew it was probably Willie's bird. So, Joe brought her over to Willie. Willie was embarrassed that one of his prize-winning birds decided to make a pit stop and visit the neighbors on the way home.

As we started working out, in the middle of a set of curls Joe said, "Bernstein, you are a fucking genius! Good work my man! My mom and dad are letting me go on the trip! Whatever you said worked. You are good!" I didn't let on that I hardly said a word and that Mary did all the talking. But I took the credit anyway.

Plans were made that day to go down to Eddie's bike shop and get Joe a new bike and all his gear. I guess in the last couple of years Schwinn changed. I'm not sure of the details but Eddie said he couldn't get the Continental and bikes were not made in America anymore. So, Joe's mother bought him a model called the World Traveler. Not a bad bike, but definitely not a Continental. No chrome fork, no metallic luster in the paint. It was lighter but basically still a decent bike.

We got all the gear. Eddie was so happy I brought in a new customer, he gave Mary a nice discount, and he gave me one of those pull chain sirens that worked off your tire. The cops outlawed those things because they sounded so much like an emergency vehicle. Eddie told me he had a bunch of them and to not use it when I saw cops around.

Me and Joe started our training rides right away. He definitely was rusty, but at least he could keep his balance and before long he was able to keep up with me. I taught him all about the gears and how to use them. He had a hard time remembering not to shift on a hill and to shift only when you were pedaling. After a couple of weeks, he was a good rider.

To train for our trip we loaded up the barbells and went to the Bronx Botanical Garden, about two miles away. I used to take Wolf there to run around. My idea was to have grass and trees and bugs and little animals just like we would experience on our trip through New England on our way to Canada. We were getting into great bike shape.

Mary was nervous. Although she knew how important this trip was going to be for her Joey, she more than once needed to check in with me to make sure I knew what I was doing. By that time, I had all the maps laid out of all the states and all our routes highlighted in yellow marker. I took Joe down to get his AYH card and I drew out all the hostels we were going to stay at. He wanted nothing to do with the planning. He left that up to me, which was fine. I studied the maps and committed our itinerary to memory.

As our July 5th departure date approached, there was a lot of buzz in the neighborhood about the big trip. All Joe's friends were talking about it and wishing him well and told Joe to make sure to send post cards.

Joe's mom and dad invited me over for dinner and gave me the final onceover to make sure I knew what I was doing. I'll always remember going into their little house with the narrow hallway and off the front door, to the left, the living room with so many photos of Joe and Nicky growing up. Two blonde-haired twins through so many stages of their lives. Happy pictures of what appeared to be a fun-filled childhood, playing in the backyard, holding Spider, Joe on what must have been his cousin's bike, photos like that.

Seeing this collection of family photos so proudly displayed made me wonder why there were no family photos displayed in my house. Ever. The photos we did have stopped when Amy was about three and I was just a baby, when my old man went over the line to full-blown alcoholism. I recently asked my mother about the total absence of family photos. She said she just wanted to remember the happy times before I was born, when my father was sober.

Both Mary and Joe Sr. discussed the trip with me in detail and made me promise that Joe would call every day. I felt like I was Joe's camp counselor or a teacher, or some other adult figure, the way they were talking with me. I guess that must have been how I came off. I didn't get any questions or discussion about the trip at my house. It never occurred to me to ask for permission or money. The only thing my mother did do was call Aunt Bea to tell her I was coming up for a visit on a bike with my friend Joe. Aunt Bea told her she was crazy to let me go. The only thing my old man said was, "Remember, don't be away too long. You gotta get back to work."

That whole week before the trip, me and Joe packed and unpacked our saddlebags several times. We tried to lighten them up but somehow they kept getting heavier and heavier. I remember Joe insisting that we take a tent and sleeping bags. He promised they were light and could be rolled up really small. I told him we were hosteling and didn't need them but if he wanted them that he would have to pack them on his bike. Somehow he did.

On the fourth of July we had major fireworks in the street. Richard almost got seriously hurt after I handed him a Roman candle which he held the wrong way so the fire hit him right in the belly. Scary. Stupid. My fault. I felt terrible. We threw out the rest of the fireworks I had bought. She made me throw them in the tub and run water all over them. Twenty bucks, literally down the drain.

It was Independence Day and that's just how I was starting to feel. Free. Nobody knew what I had up my sleeve. I figured I'd tell Joe I was running away some time after Montreal when we were on our way home. The trip was going to end in Boston where I would put Joe on a bus and I would keep going. That was the plan.

CHAPTER SEVEN

FREEDOM RIDE

Early on the morning of July 5, 1971, me and Joe hit the road. I wheeled my loaded-up Schwinn Continental out of the garage and headed over to Joe's house. Mary was crying. Nicky was hung over but cheering us on. Joe Sr. had already gone to work. Mary fed us a hearty breakfast of pancakes and sausages. My family had already said good-bye to me the night before.

Me and Joe took off after breakfast. We went down Allerton to Boston Post Road and headed north. It was perfect. The sun was already bright, it was Monday and Independence Day was being celebrated so traffic was light. I led, Joe followed. The first town we hit right out of The Bronx was New Rochelle on the way to our final destination for the day, a place called Squantz Pond State Park, about sixty miles away in Connecticut. Sixty miles was a lot for our first day, considering that our Botanical

Garden training rides amounted to no more than fifteen miles. But, we were up for it. Since there would be no youth hostels until we hit Massachusetts, Joe was happy he was going to get to use his camping gear at the state park.

It's Day One, we are cruising along on the Boston Post Road north and just hit New Rochelle. I had already gotten used to Joe's constant jabbering, mostly about how hot it was or that he was hungry or that a tractor trailer almost hit him. Stuff like that. I tuned most of it out.

We were only twenty minutes into our trip when I realized I had stopped hearing Joe's whining. I glanced back, but didn't see him. I was thinking, *don't tell me he got run over or took a wrong turn so early in our trip*. I circled around and about a quarter of a mile back, there was Joe stopped on the side of the road kicking his bike and screaming his Italian curses at it. He got a flat. Not only had we been riding for only a few minutes and already had a problem, it dawned on me that one of the things I had failed to do was teach Joe how to fix a flat, or, for that matter, any basic repairs. It was getting hot and I figured that this was going to be a very long day. Joe stripped his bike of all its gear and flipped it upside down. Then he took a seat on the curb as I showed him how to repair his first flat tire but I'm not sure how much attention he was paying. He never fixed a single flat or did any of the other repairs I showed him how to do, but he always cheered me on. Just like he didn't want any part of planning the trip, bike repair didn't much interest him. Same with keeping on the lookout for road signs. Map reading. Same with cooking. Mostly, he was in it for all those girls we were going to meet on the road.

That first day was a bitch. Between the heat and the trucks and the fumes and our blistering butts, Joe and I persevered until we got to our destination. A credit to our toughness. My carefully chosen routes not only kept us off the major highways but took us through beautiful New England countryside through the hills of Connecticut. Those hills killed us. Back in the planning stages we were thinking Connecticut would be an easy warm-up. There are no Green or White Mountains in Connecticut like when you hit New Hampshire and Vermont. First day out, after the flat tire, since we weren't on the major roads, it seemed like nothing but hills. The Botanical Garden was a cakewalk compared to this ride.

I had packed about two pounds of granola trail mix that I made up the day before the trip. It was a recipe right out of the hostel guide book for stamina and energy for those long, hot rides. Well, we had ourselves one. The whining and jabbering started up again two or three miles after the flat in New Rochelle. I think the main reason for the whining was that Joe hadn't really experienced much hardship in his life and was used to a more comfortable lifestyle. It's not that I enjoyed hardship, I was just more used to it. The whining wasn't because of a lack of toughness. After a few days, the whining turned into just regular everyday jabbering. At that point we got used to the aches and pains, got into real bike shape, and started to enjoy the trip.

But not this day. It was hell. Joe pleaded to take the next few days off rather than, as planned, first thing the next morning hitting the road up to our first hostel in Springfield, Massachusetts. I totally agreed. All I could think of was getting to the campsite and crashing. Food wasn't an issue. We had our fill of trail mix and somewhere around forty miles in we lost our appetites. On the other hand, we couldn't keep enough water in us. We went through our three canteens every hour or so and had to stop at gas stations and the occasional McDonald's to fill up.

Aside from the flat tire, considering it was our first day and I totally overestimated our riding abilities and underestimated the terrain, the trip took about four hours more than expected. Instead of rolling in at six, we crept in at ten. I burnt out my first set of batteries in the new headlamp I bought from Eddie's just about when we saw the sign for the state park. It's a good thing the moon was bright that night. Me and Joe got off our bikes, congratulated each other with a handshake and a hug, had a few swigs of water, and stretched our legs and butts. It was so painful to walk that we hopped back on the bikes and meandered around looking for the campsites.

After about a half hour of almost pitch black riding and not seeing any more signs for the campground, Joe, being much more familiar with camping than me, said,

"You know, maybe this whole thing is the campgrounds. Maybe we can pitch the tent anywhere!"

"Let's do it!" I said. We were so dead tired, me and Joe had just about no energy left to set up his tent at the foot of a knoll, unroll the sleeping bags, and crash.

We slept soundly until about eight the next morning. In my dreamy mind, I thought I was hearing roosters crowing. Not that I ever heard them before in my life but it made sense in my sleepy head that the sun comes up, you're in the country, and the rooster goes cock-a-doodle-doo. Right? Not so right.

Not only that, it didn't smell too good. We were so exhausted the night before we hadn't noticed, but it was like somebody left an open bag of rotting garbage out in your kitchen for a few days, but much stronger.

As the not-rooster crowed, there was also digging outside at the edge of the tent. I got a little alarmed so I elbowed Joe, who was snoring away, and I decided he was not going to be of much help. I grabbed my hand pump which I pulled into the tent with all my gear the night before and got ready to go out cautiously to see what was going on with all the noise and scratching and digging. I heard the sound again and realized that the noise was not cock-a-doodle-doo but howling and yelping. Again, not really sounds I was very familiar with although it was reminiscent of dogs. But this sound was different enough to make the hair on the back of my neck go up. Joe was still snoring away.

So, here's what I saw when I opened up the flap of the tent, just a couple of inches: four coyotes. Two were circling and sniffing around the tent and two were scratching to get in. I realized they must be after the trail mix. Maybe. They didn't appear too ominous to me, kind of like small, thin, tannish, shepherd-mix type dogs, but definitely wild. They were yelping and howling and talking to the rest of their family. Three more coyotes came down over the knoll. Just like the coyotes were not a rooster, the knoll was not a knoll.

We had been so tired and in such pain our first night and couldn't see six inches in front of us that taking Joe's suggestion that we were already in the campground sounded good. Instead of the campground, we had pitched our tent at the foot of a landfill, loaded with coyotes. Come to find out, we had been riding around in circles and never even made it to the campgrounds. It was more than two miles away.

I zipped up the flap, woke Joe up, and told him about our predicament. We started making a lot of racket and punching the side-walls. Eventually the coyotes lost interest and ran off. We probably broke the record for how fast it took to get dressed, collapse a tent, load up our bikes, and hightail it out of that garbage dump.

We made it to the actual campsite in twenty minutes, repitched the tent, decided to take the day off, and slept until dinner time. We finished off the trail mix and found a diner where we ate pretty much nonstop. The next morning, we hit the road for the huge International Youth Hostel in Springfield, Massachusetts. Although we were looking forward to our hostel, I was particularly interested in the Basketball Hall of Fame museum in downtown Springfield.

The ride to Springfield proved to be a lot further than our first day to Squantz Pond, but it was flatter and, more importantly, we were rested. We left about eight in the morning and made it to Route 5 outside of Hartford by one in the afternoon. By four we were checking in to the International Youth Hostel. Again, due to the heat, the traffic, the trucks, the hills and small roads, Joe and I were beat. To his credit, Joe, knowing we had a big ride in front of us, hardly complained at all. This ride put us into bike shape that carried us throughout the trip. All told, the mileage that day was somewhere over seventy but seemed so much less.

When we got in, we showed our AYH cards, and found the men's dorms and settled in for a long nap. The hostel was gigantic and just about empty.

Thank God there was an all-night White Castle open when we woke up around eight. We got our usual dozen or so half-dollar sized burgers, stringy fries, and soupy shakes. Heaven. We went back to the empty hostel and slept it all off.

The next day the hostel wasn't empty anymore. Kids with bikes and gear were flooding in. Me and Joe checked out license plates and counted cars from six different states pulling in and out to drop them off. Moms and dads unloading teens and bikes and saddlebags, hugging and kissing and tears and goodbyes all around. Dozens of families. Just watching the comings and goings provided us with entertainment all afternoon.

One girl came up with her parents in a giant Ford station wagon with New York plates. She was short and cute. Our eyes locked in for just a moment. We smiled at each other and I had a feeling I'd be seeing her again.

Me and Joe stayed in Springfield for two nights. As with all hostels, the cost was about three bucks a night and included a bunk in a dorm and total access to the kitchen. There were always bathroom facilities with showers and sometimes cool attractions in the area like swimming lakes, movie theaters, scenic mountains and, in this town, the Basketball Hall of Fame.

After a few hours of watching kids with bikes and crying moms, me and Joe rode down to a Western Union office and, happily, shipped all his bulky camping gear back home. Our next stop was the Basketball Hall of Fame. For me, this was a dream of a lifetime. I almost expected the Harlem Globetrotters to meet us at the door twirling basketballs on their fingertips and throwing buckets of confetti at us. Instead the place was empty and eerily quiet. The short guy who took our fifty cents at the entry door wore a dark blue suit with brass buttons, a white button down shirt, and a red tie. Very official. He didn't crack a smile.

I looked around at all the basketball paraphernalia and newspaper clippings and photographs of the players on the walls. There were biographies and stats on all the famous players throughout the history of the game. A hoop and backboard was set low about six feet off the floor and right in front of it was a poster and stat sheet of one of the game's all-time greats, Wilt "The Stilt" Chamberlain. On a table, right in front of Chamberlain's poster, along with his jersey and his size 18 sneakers, was the original basketball he had played with on that day in 1962 when he scored 100 points for the Philadelphia Warriors against the New York Knicks. Not the same Knicks as the ones I was in love with in 1971. My Knicks had beat Chamberlain for the championship in the 1969–70 NBA championship series, with what I consider the best team in the history of the NBA: Willis Reed, Walt Frazier, Dave DeBusschere, Dick Barnett, and Bill Bradley. It was that famous final Game Seven when Willis Reed came limping out of the locker room with a torn thigh muscle and scored the game's first four points. That moment is indelibly marked on my brain as the greatest sports moment in my life. Reed, through his toughness and courage, led his Knicks to their first NBA championship against the Chamberlain-led Lakers.

I was in awe, staring at the leather basketball that Chamberlain had used to do the unimaginable. Usually a 20- or 30-point game from a player is admirable. The Stilt scored 100!

Yes, Chamberlain was taller and stronger than any-body in the game before, during, and, some say, since. The teams he played for revolved their offense around him. He hardly ever played less than forty-eight minutes, in other words he was on the court the whole game. In later years, as he slowed down, Chamberlain focused his skills on defense and again, utilizing his superior physi-cality, dominated the floor. Still, all that said, 100 points from one guy is an amazing feat. One that has never been matched in the history of the sport.

The guy at the door with the brass buttons was nowhere to be found so Joe, upon seeing my wonder-ment with Wilt the Stilt's ball, picked it up and started dribbling it. He said " Yo, Bernstein, here, take the shot of your life," as he passed it towards the hoop for me to grab and lay in. As I saw the ball flying through the air, I leapt and caught it and, in one fluid motion, dunked it through the hoop. I never could have done that on a reg-ulation-sized hoop. Well, with all the racket of Joe yell-ing and me going for the alley-oop and, unfortunately, knocking over some display items as I sailed through the air, Mr. Brass Buttons showed up. I apologized and Joe laughed as Mr. Buttons grabbed the ball and pointed to the door. He didn't say a word. He never did.

Back at the Springfield hostel, Joe and I decided to see if we could find some girls to talk to. Well, truth be told, he asked if I could find them and then he would join in. Sure enough, with all the kids checking in, more than half were girls. It seemed like it should be easy to charm one or two, after all we were two tough guys from "Da Bronx." Everyone else was from New Jersey, Connecticut, Long Island, or Westchester County. Suburbanites.

A long table was set up in the main lobby for paperwork and group registration. Joe and I sat down. From our seats at the center of the table, we figured we'd have the best vantage point to scope out the girls as they arrived. We also hoped it would make it seem like we were in charge.

Right away that girl who had caught my eye earlier caught the other one too. She was really pretty, shortish, long brown hair, had a friendly smile, and was very well proportioned. She smiled at me again. We started talking.

Joe gave me a nudge and whispered in my ear, "Don't forget about me, Bernstein." I ignored him and paid a lot of attention to the girl smiling and batting her eyelashes at me.

I asked her, "So what's all this about? What are all you guys doin' here?" She told me this is the place groups meet and get organized and hit the road from. The way she talked was way different than girls I was used to. No real accent, be it Bronxese or Spanish or Southern. She sounded and seemed what I thought of as sophisticated. She told me she was from Long Island, a place called Sands Point.

"So, did you meet your group?" I asked.

"A few of them, but some aren't here yet."

"How many of you are there?"

"About ten of us. We're going up to Canada." And then she was like a machine gun, firing out questions and comments. "So, who are you? Where did you come from? Where are you going? What kind of group are you with? How many of you are there? Did your parents drive you here? How old are you? My name is Gina."

"My name is Steve. I rode up with my friend Joe, the guy who keeps butting in, whispering crap in my ear and annoying me. We're from The Bronx and we're going to Montreal to visit my Aunt Bea."

Our eyes locked while we were talking. Not only were her questions rapid fired, she smiled the whole time she was talking. I liked her. I felt easy with her despite her lack of accent. The third time Joe came over and nudged me, I introduced him to Gina.

She said. "Wow! Two guys from The Bronx! This could be exciting! Maybe you can join our group!"

Me and Joe looked at each other and then sized Gina up, looked at each other again and simultaneously said, "No way." Joe added, "We're independents."

In talking to Gina, I started to think that once in a while it would be fun to see someone else on the road besides Joe. Even though I grew to love the guy, he was at times obnoxious and boy wouldn't it be nice to see some curves now and then other than the ones on the road?

A very tall, slim, curly-haired blonde young woman with a great smile came over to us and saw Gina's name tag and introduced herself as the leader of her group. "Hi, my name is Belinda," she said and shook Gina's hand and then looked at me and Joe and asked, "Are you guys with us, too?"

Joe piped up, "No, we're independents."

Then Gina chimed in, "This is Steve and Joe, they're from The Bronx." Belinda shook our hands and smiled. "They're going to Canada just like us, maybe they can tag along, right Belinda?"

Belinda, being at least 6-foot-2, towered over all of us, especially Gina who was barely five feet tall, and just smiled and said, "We'll see."

Joe gave me another nudge after Gina and Belinda left and said, "Bernstein, we ain't tagging along with nobody!" He was about to say more when he stopped himself short, reconsidered and said, "Well, if there are other cute girls like Gina in the group, maybe we can kind of follow along. You know, keep tabs on them from a distance."

I saw several kids finding their way to the part of the table where Belinda and Gina were signing kids in. Gina waved us over and introduced us all around as everybody was getting acquainted. Every time she introduced us, about ten times, Gina motioned towards us and said, "And this is Steve and Joe, they're from The Bronx. They're independents."

I elbowed Joe and whispered, "Keep an open mind, take my lead, and don't talk too much."

There were a lot of confused faces, but in a short time the kids in the group all realized that we weren't an official part of the group, because we were on our own, being independents and all. I don't remember all their names but a girl with glasses and dark, curly hair started making googly-eyes towards Joe. Her name was Cecilia. All that night and for the rest of the fucking trip, I had to listen to an off-key version of Simon and Garfunkel's song "Cecilia." Especially the part when Paul sang, "I got up to wash my face, when I got back to bed someone's taken my place . . . Cecilia!!!" Joe told me he was in love. Pathetic.

Me and Joe hit the road the next day and ended up in Sunderland, Massachusetts. Compared to the first two days of riding, this ride was a vacation. On the way from Springfield to Sunderland, a straight shot more or less of about thirty miles of pretty flat riding, we passed through a cool town called Amherst. There was a farmer's market and an old-fashioned movie theater playing old-fashioned movies. That week, it was *Casablanca*. There were some funky bookstores and three Chinese restaurants all in one block! Me and Joe treated ourselves to lunch at one of them. Right next door was a little drugstore with a soda fountain counter that also sold penny candy. For dessert, we each had an egg cream and, for the first time on our trip, we got some postcards and mailed them home. I bought one with a photo of the Amherst Common and Joe bought ten. He said, "I got a lot of people I told I was gonna keep in touch with, besides they were ten for a buck, so why not?"

In Sunderland, we stayed in an old but beautifully maintained farmhouse. Upstairs in the attic, one flight up from our dorm, lived an older guy with no teeth named Granville. He was short and skinny and really quite friendly but the hostel parent said don't bother making conversation with Granville; he's mute. That didn't stop Joe who got Granville laughing at all his corny jokes. Next thing you know Granville joined in as Joe sang "Cecilia" off-key. Then Granville started talking. He told us that he had lived in Sunderland all his life and the hostel parents took him in at some point as their groundskeeper. He brought us apples from the orchards where he worked and offered us his hand-rolled cigarettes from the tobacco farm nearby.

The group made it to Sunderland the next day. I started spending a lot of time with Gina and left Joe to fend for himself. Me and Gina laughed and talked and found each other to be quite compatible. There was a strong friendship forming as well as a romance. We rode our bikes to a nearby lake called Lake Wyola where we laid down our hostel towels on the sandy beach and swam to the floating dock. We did a whole lot of talking. Well, Gina did most of the talking, but I was a great listener. And we kissed. On the dock and on the beach. And, on the lips.

Putney, Vermont, was next. Again, an easy ride, straight up Route 5 about thirty-five miles from Sunderland. Riding up Route 5 ran parallel to the Connecticut River so the riding was easy because it was flat.

Up to that point, we had met some interesting people, had some fun adventures, hooked up with this cool
group, and I had a cute main squeeze. But nothing prepared us for what we encountered in Putney. You have to
understand, this was 1971: hippies, weed, anti-war pro-
tests, flags and bras were burning.

Now, me and Joe were sixteen, from The Bronx, so there
really wasn't that much consciousness being raised about
countercultural movements in our immediate environment.
Not that it wasn't going on, but just not in our immediate
awareness. For example, Ben, Amy's new husband, leaned
towards hippieness. That became evident to me because he
used words like "cool," "far out," and "groovy," but most
obvious was the consistent availability of hash in their
apartment. Hippieness just wasn't my cup of tea.

While the hippies avoided the draft and were out pro-
testing against the war, my friends a few years older than
me were coming home in body bags from the "Vietnam
conflict." A few years later I became a draft dodger. Joe
couldn't wait to turn eighteen and get his draft card.

Most of what I knew about hippies was related to pro-
testing the war. That all changed when Joe and I rolled
into Putney. We got to the hostel address, took one look
at the house, and kept on riding, certain we had the
wrong address. Finally, we realized we did have the right
address but it sure looked like the wrong house.

Unlike the manicured old farmhouse in Sunderland,
this old farmhouse was dilapidated. It had white peeling

paint, a collapsed side roof, a rotting wooden porch, crab grass for a lawn, a God-awful smelling barrel with flies buzzing all around it in the front yard which I later learned was the compost bin, a rusted out '60 Chevy pickup raised up on blocks with the hood up and no wheels and, of course, in the driveway a Volkswagen van with flowers painted all over it.

We rode into the driveway next to the van, got off our bikes, put the kickstands down, took a swig of water, looked at each other with some apprehension, and walked up the rickety porch steps to the front door.

I had my hostel pass and guide book in one hand and knocked with the other. Joe cowered behind me. I was ready to either not get an answer or maybe some gruff motorcycle gang guys would be there and me and Joe would have to figure out our next move. Fast. After two knocks the door opened. Standing in the doorway was this beautiful very pale, blue-eyed young woman nursing a baby at her naked breast. She had long, dark hair down her back, a tie-dyed tank top pulled down below her breasts, faded blue denim bell-bottom jeans, and sandals.

I hesitated for a moment before I was able to inquire if we were at the right place. Behind me I heard Joe gasp and stumble backwards off the steps. The Putney hostel was a commune. Communes were a way of life in Vermont at that time.

The young woman introduced herself as Laura and the baby was Hendrix. Hendrix was cute and round and happy.

Joe regained his composure and I introduced us; I told her we were riding up from The Bronx to Montreal. Laura smiled and welcomed us inside. In order to keep Joe from staring at Laura and Hendrix, I kept him busy unloading our gear and finding our bunks while I signed us in.

"I guess you guys don't see too much of this down in The Bronx?" Laura asked. I wasn't exactly sure what she was referring to, her breasts and Hendrix or the commune. "Yeah, we been living off the land here for a couple of years. There's lots of us up here in this area. I'm originally from New Jersey. I couldn't walk around like this, with Hendrix. They'd arrest me. We trade labor for rent and there's eleven of us living here."

As I was listening and checking the place out, I commented to myself, *I wouldn't pay rent either for this dump.* Peeling, stained wallpaper, moldy rugs, soiled diapers in various piles, broken furniture, an old couch with springs popping out of the bottom, and a stench in the air of urine, pot, and baby poo. Arlo, a big old bloodhound, was laying in between the springs on the crappy couch. "That's great, Laura, imagine what this would cost in New Jersey?" I was trying to be nice. At least Hendrix was happy and Laura was free to express herself.

She pointed out the back window in the kitchen and said, "The boys will be in soon, after they hay the field." A bunch of shirtless guys with long hair and beards were chasing an old pickup truck as they were loading bales of hay into the back.

"Groovy," I said. Me and Joe had a mellow evening hanging out with the hippies. They all turned out to be gentle people, mostly from the New York area, working hard, trying to make a go of this farm. Funny how each one of them was either a college graduate or a dropout. They were unhappy with the war, the status quo, and their parents who, for the most part, were professionals of some sort and had money but, according to this crew, were fake and unhappy.

As I took a few puffs of weed that night, I told the hippies about my life. Joe couldn't take his eyes off of Laura. Laura's man didn't seem to mind, though. After I shared my story, I was invited to move in and join them. They had sympathy for my situation. Plus, I had some skills.

Bobby, Laura's husband, teared up when I told him some of the adventures I had gone through in The Bronx. Of course, the hash he was smoking probably exaggerated his emotions.

He said, "I thought I had it bad when my old man told me if I didn't come into the family car business, he would cut my allowance off. So, I had to leave. But, you, you've had some serious shit to deal with, son. At least you're learning a trade."

I said "Bobby, I learned I gotta do what I gotta do. My family is doin' okay now. I'm on vacation. Maybe permanently."

Bobby pointed to the stain on the ceiling and asked, "Any chance you can fix that leaky pipe? I'll give you and your boy here," motioning to Joe who was sleeping next to Arlo, "a free night and a full breakfast on the house."

"Sure, no problem."

Putney was an education. The people were laid back and kind. They seemed to be on a mission. By meeting them, I was able to fill in some gaps in my understanding about what the hippies were all about. I knew being a hippie had something to do with being anti-war, escaping their parents' attitudes and values, finding peace, living off the land. Being free. It resonated with so much of what I was starting to feel. I didn't think I could live with all the distractions commune life posed, though, namely all the drugs and exposed breasts, but I did find myself liking a lot of what they were trying to accomplish.

The next morning at 5:30, I woke up to Bobby nudging my arm with a pipe wrench in his hand. The aroma of pancakes and sausages was in the air. Bobby asked, "You ready to do some plumbing, man?"

I fixed the leak and woke Joe up for that hearty breakfast while outside the clouds were getting very dark. As we were eating, Bobby looked over at me, and then outside at the dilapidated shed roof and said, "We got a big rain coming, do you know anything about leaky roofs?" I lied and told him my experience was limited to pipes.

Laura and Hendrix were at it again. Joe was useless. I told Laura about a bike group that was coming this way today from Sunderland, Massachusetts. She had already heard from Belinda and was preparing the two large dorms for them. Joe and I decided to hang around and wait for the group. Me, so I could see Gina and Joe, so he could see more of Laura's mammaries.

It started to drizzle just as Belinda and the ten bikers arrived. The group was elated that they had missed the storm. They dumped their bikes and gear in the barn and piled into the kitchen through the side door. Everyone except Gina. She had seen me standing on the front porch looking for her. Her legs, socks, and sneakers were splattered with mud. He hair was damp and stuck to her forehead from a combination of drizzle and sweat. She looked beautiful to me. We exchanged a grimy hug and a kiss, as the drizzle turned into rain.

The group's plan was to go from Putney to North Haverhill, New Hampshire, with no more than one overnight at each hostel on the way. Unfortunately, a storm was coming and the group wouldn't be able to go anywhere. They were stuck in Putney for at least two days.

The group had a rigidly fixed itinerary. Nights were booked and paid for in advance. This meant that every day was critical and the group had to make it to their scheduled hostel each night or risk losing their reservation in the busy summer months. Especially if it was a large group like this one.

Belinda was going crazy trying to figure out how to keep her group on schedule. They were headed up to North Haverhill, New Hampshire, about a hundred miles north. Because of the time lost due to the storm, she knew they would never make it to the two hostels on the way.

The group's scheduled stops could fall like dominos, one hostel after the other. It made me grateful that me and Joe, being independents as we were, hardly worried about schedules.

The urgency of this logistical challenge became clear late that second evening. Belinda was crying as she rolled a joint from the hippies' communal stash. She told me she would drive the group if only she knew how. I looked at her and said, "You kiddin? Will that solve your problem? I been drivin' for years." She looked at me, smiled, and gave me a big hug.

That next morning Bobby gave me, Joe, Gina, and Belinda a ride in his VW camper to the gas station in downtown Putney. Belinda used travelers checks to rent us a sixteen-foot moving truck.

I was worried, seeing as how I was the only one with a license. Well, sort of a license. My little paper permit card was temporary until I went to a DMV to get a permanent license. It said PERMIT right across the top of the card. The guy in the gas station couldn't have cared less. He had no problem renting a moving truck to a sixteen-year-old with a questionable temporary New York license. Putney was real laid back to say the least.

When we got back to the commune, it was still pouring. The group began packing up and Gina joined Laura in the kitchen making sandwiches for the road.

Me and Joe had grown to feel very accepted and comforted by this loving and sweet family. It even got to be no big deal seeing naked breasts. I'm not sure if it was because we were getting used to persistent partial nudity or if it was the buzz of the pot in the air that mellowed us out. The hippie family was genuinely sorry to see us all take off. Especially me and Joe. After our three days in the commune, we felt like family. There was peace and acceptance in this falling-down farmhouse. Sure was different than my family.

Belinda was elated that she had found a way to get back on course but she hadn't exactly told the group the whole story, how they were going to travel in the pouring rain the hundred miles from Putney, Vermont, to North Haverhill, New Hampshire. Standing in the driveway wearing their plastic rain ponchos, with their bagged lunches in one hand and their saddle bags in the other, the group took one look at that moving truck backed up to the barn, a big box body with no windows and a roll-up door. They begged not to be put inside it.

Belinda explained that there was no other way and that the trip would end early if they didn't get up to North Haverhill. Reluctantly, they all piled in to the back of the truck. Me and Joe loaded the bikes in after them. I made a deal with Belinda that if I was driving, Joe was shotgun and Gina would squeeze in on the big bench seat between us.

Damn! Was I scared! Here I was not even seventeen yet, driving a truck full of kids and bikes through winding mountain roads for a hundred miles in the pouring rain. Gina sensed I was nervous and said, "Look at the bright side, at least we got seats!"

Joe, being the gentleman, gave up his seat and moved to the back several times to give Belinda and then most of the group a break from retching or passing out from the fumes and lack of air. Every twenty minutes, I stopped to let one green and nauseous kid into the cab and sent the other, somewhat less green kid, back to the rear of the truck. It made me grateful that I was the driver. A little.

The truck was no sports car and negotiating those winding Vermont mountainous roads in the pouring rain was no easy task. I tried to keep the ride as smooth as possible, but with each curve I felt and heard the groans and thumps of teenagers, bikes, and saddle bags crashing into each other. With each hill, either up or down, I had to downshift, causing the truck to buck. Thank God I had had all that practice driving my old man around The Bronx the last few years. The Bronx, with traffic lights and straight streets was one thing, these country roads were quite another. My old man's '67 green Dodge Sportsman van was an Alfa Romeo compared to this monster. Thankfully I had Joe for much of the trip singing "Cecilia" off key and Gina telling me how great I was doing.

I had the lives of all these people on my shoulders. I wished someone could have helped me with the fear I wasn't showing and the nervous cramps in my gut and the tension in my arms and neck I wasn't complaining about. The curves, the hills, the mountains, the miles, and that rain never seemed to end. I wasn't about to back down from a tough situation. They were all counting on me.

We pulled into the Lime Kiln Road Hostel in North Haverhill about seven in the evening. The rain had finally stopped. Everybody unloaded out of the back, sick and exhausted but relieved that we had made it. The group, except for Gina and Belinda, found their rooms and crashed for the night. Nobody felt much like eating, except, as usual, me and Joe. We were famished. Not surprisingly there were still about fifteen untouched peanut butter and jelly sandwiches on Wonder bread that Gina and Laura had made. Gina had slipped a pickle into the sandwich she gave me and told me that's how they do it on the North Shore.

Miraculously, nobody died or even stayed sick. Everybody settled in to the hostel, which was an old house with a bunch of little cabins built around it. The four of us, tired and still on edge from the crazy day, sat around the faded Formica kitchen table talking. The kitchen had a wood stove for both cooking and heat, a noisy thirty-year-old refrigerator, exposed brass water pipes, and a wet and moldy smell. Belinda broke into her stash and lit up a joint. She was obviously starting to realize how utterly insane it was to have done that drive and, at the same time, she was ecstatic that it had all worked out. Almost.

Belinda passed around the joint and the three of us declined, thank God. Little did I know I would still need my faculties intact that night. Right then I said, "Hey, Belinda, since we're staying here a few days, I'm sleeping late, so don't bother me too early to bring the truck to town to return it, okay?"

Belinda jumped up, knocking over her metal kitchen chair, the joint flew across the room, she put her hands to her curly hair and started to pull at it. She yelled, "Holy fuckin' shit! I just remembered when I filled out the papers at the U-Haul place in Putney, they said it was going to have to be round trip! There is no place up here to return it!"

Not knowing much about these things, I had to process this information for a minute. So, I asked, "Does that mean we have to take it back?"

"Yeah," she said.

"And then how do we get back?" I asked.

"I guess we'll have to hitch."

I didn't want to deal with anything more that day so I told her, "Okay, let me and Joe sleep late and we'll go down in the morning." Joe, half-awake but still listening, nodded. Me and Joe were turning to leave the kitchen to go to sleep for at least twelve hours out in our own little cabin just when we heard Gina ask, "Belinda? Is there more?" Joe and I turned back.

Belinda's brow was furrowed and she was tearing up. Very sheepishly, Belinda said, "Yes."

Me and Joe looked at each other, exhausted and confused, and plopped down on the metal chairs and waited for the next bit of reality that Belinda was going to lay on us. She pulled out the truck paperwork from her denim purse. Without making any eye contact, Belinda told us the truck had to be back by midnight. Tonight.

A hundred miles, wet winding Vermont mountainous roads, a moving truck, it's now a little after seven, getting dark soon, we're dead tired, I'm the only one who can drive, we have to hitch back, all this swirling around in my head and Joe pipes up, "No problem, we're on it!" I wanted to belt him.

Well, the group settled in for the night as me and Joe gobbled down some food. We climbed back into the truck ready to start back to Putney at 7:30 that night. At least the rain had stopped and I wasn't about to worry how we'd get back. I was sure we'd find a way. As I was getting the maps organized and Joe was packing some more peanut butter and jelly sandwiches and refilling our canteens for the night, Gina appeared on one side of me and Belinda on the other and both said in unison, "We're goin' with you!"

We made it back to Putney by about 10:30. I couldn't believe how much easier the return trip was even though it was pitch dark. We played the radio, told stories, Joe sang off-key and told corny jokes, Gina and Belinda joined in and we had a grand time, the four of us squeezed onto that bench seat in that big old Ford moving truck.

After returning the truck, Belinda asked the guy at the station for the best road to try and get a lift up north to North Haverhill. As he was on his way home for the night, he dropped us off about ten miles north on a main road. Belinda and Gina stuck out their thumbs trying to get a ride, while me and Joe hung back. It was now pushing eleven and hardly a car was on the road. After about a half hour a green VW bug puttered up to us and stopped. The driver rolled down the window and asked where we were heading. We told him and he said, "Well you are truly blessed tonight, my friends. That's just where I'm goin'. Hop in!"

Well, needless to say, it was a tight squeeze. Belinda with her long legs up front and me, Gina, and Joe like sardines in the back. Now if you're not familiar with that era of VW Beetles, it has several very distinct characteristics. First is its tiny, round size and shape; they don't call it a bug for nothing. Next is its rear-mounted air-cooled engine with not too much more power than a go-kart, and it sounds like a lawn mower. The forty-something horsepower engine was barely enough to move it and the driver around, let alone passengers. The air-cooled engine also had a heat exchanger that theoretically diverted warm air to the heater and defroster.

It was a warm summer night, so heat wasn't an issue. Five good-sized adults was more than this little bug could handle. The car couldn't go over twenty-five on the flat. With five adults expiring and perspiring in this sardine can, fogging up the windows on an already misty night, that heat exchanger defroster didn't have a prayer keeping the windshield clear. You can imagine how arduous it was to drive this thing. But all the above weren't the main problem.

One of the reasons the driver, maybe a thirty-year-old guy, was so friendly was because he was tripping. Later Belinda told us he had leaned over and offered her some acid.

His driving seemed fine. It was his delusions of grandeur that concerned me. Such as introducing himself to Belinda, very matter-of-factly, as Jesus Christ. He said that just that very morning he had walked on water over a pond to get to his mother's house. Well he did look the part with long hair, beard, headband, and sandals.

Belinda turned to the back seat. Joe was sleeping and I had my arm around Gina. We really couldn't hear the conservation in the front seat over the putt-putt of the straining engine. But when Belinda took her pointer finger and made a circling motion around her temple while nodding towards Jesus, Gina and I knew we may be in for a rough ride. Oddly enough, although the average speed barely broke twenty-five miles per hour and Jesus talked a mile a minute about God knows what, we made it back to Lime Kiln Road by three in the morning, relatively unscathed and ready to put this day to bed. We all thanked Jesus as he drove away and flashed us the two-finger "V" symbol for peace.

We went straight to the kitchen where we raided the ice box, found an expired Carvel ice cream cake, and pigged out sitting in those crappy metal chairs around that faded Formica table. Belinda took me and Gina on the side and gave us her blessing. She told us we could have our own cabin. Joe couldn't have cared less at that point. He was so tired, he was already snoring on the couch in the living room.

It certainly was a memorable day. And night.

After North Haverhill, there were about six more hostels winding up the Connecticut River on our way to Montreal. Me and Joe pretty much traveled right along with the group. To maintain our independent status, we took an extra night here or there or chose a slightly different route, but all in all we were Joe and Steve, the tough guys from The Bronx. We were as much a part of that group as any of those rich kids who welcomed us with open arms and said they missed us when we weren't around. Me and Joe were trying, but not too hard, to maintain our status as the "independents."

After Joe bragged about how experienced a bike mechanic I was, I had kids lining up for seat adjustments, gear adjustments, chain repairs, brake adjustments, pumping up tires, and flat repairs almost daily. You have to remember this was before the days of quick-release wheels and seats as well as all the modern technology we have on bikes these days. So, that dog bone wrench and my pliers and screwdriver were pretty much it for tools. It was all good, I enjoyed being the fix-it guy.

Biking forty-five miles a day got me and Joe into good biking shape. But it wasn't enough for us; we missed our garage ironman workouts. So, every day after the ride or sometimes during the ride, we took push-up and sit-up breaks. Call us crazy, we didn't want to leave any muscle group out. After all, we had met the year before, competing head to head in a push-up competition. It was fun to keep score, but we didn't care who won. We were always neck and neck.

The effect of our ironman workout didn't go unnoticed by Gina. She dubbed me Captain Body and even made me a T-shirt with a Captain Body logo. She was a fantastic artist and I still have that T-shirt.

After North Haverhill and our own private cabin, and the wild U-Haul ride through the mountains, the rest of the trip to Canada settled into a laid-back sightseeing trip. We all had a lot of fun. We had been on the road about three weeks and had ridden around 250 miles all told. Me and Gina got closer, friends as well as romance close. Joe was really enjoying himself being a tough guy, a comedian, and having the attention of the other girls, especially Cecilia, along with the guys who looked up to him in awe of his Bronx bravado.

Even with all the romance and sightseeing and goofing around and adventures we had had tagging along with this group all the way up to Canada, I never let go of my original plan. As much as I was having the time of my life, I was still ready to run away, move on, not go back.

There'd be a moment, with just me and Joe, when I would explain to him that I wasn't going back. He'd understand. He'd be happy for me. We hadn't known each other that long, almost two years by then, but he knew me, he knew my life. He witnessed it. So often, in his own way, he had tried to comfort me when shit was going down for me at home.

I wasn't sure Gina would understand. She hardly knew about me and my real life. At fifteen, she saw what she saw, what she wanted to see. More to the point what I showed her: Captain Body.

The border crossing into Canada was a breeze. One lone Canadian border guard came out of what looked like one lone toll booth and waved us through. He didn't even ask us for our passports, which was a good thing because me and Joe didn't have any.

After two more days on the road, we finally made it to downtown Montreal where we stayed at a hostel located in the YMCA near McGill University. The hostel parent seemed nice enough, short, bald, and round with a handlebar mustache. He knew no English so we couldn't converse too well, but I got the gist of what he was saying. I was hoping Gina and the crowd would arrive soon to help with the French. All I knew was Spanish and Joe was limited to Italian curse words. He made fun of the hostel parent and nicknamed him Alphonse.

For some reason, the Y was empty and me and Joe had the run of the place. We used the pool, the weight room, played basketball—it was like a private summer camp for us. One hundred percent freedom. Except for Alphonse.

He and Joe did not hit it off. Joe with his Irish-Italian-Bronx accent tried talking to Alphonse and must have hit a nerve. For a couple of days, we walked on eggshells while we waited for the group to arrive. Everything we did, whether it was accidentally setting off fire alarms, or crashing the barbells, or horsing around in the pool, or using too many towels, or messing up the kitchen with greasy, smoky food, Alphonse gave us shit. Thank God, the group was only two days behind us.

Me and Joe took advantage of those two days to get to know the city. Right around McGill University, near the Y, it felt like home. Tall buildings. A subway. Taxis and Chinese restaurants. People of many ethnicities.

Yet there were some key differences compared to New York City. The streets were busy, yes, but quiet. And clean. No horns honking. No blaring music. No overflowing trash, litter flying around, or piles of dog shit on the side-walk. The air even smelled better than in New York.

The biggest difference was the look on people's faces. Even though they were on their way to school, work, maybe shopping, they didn't look anxious. They were calm. New Yorkers are edgy and afraid, always in a hurry, like they are racing from or to something. But the people on these Montreal city streets seemed content.

The group showed up. Gina went to work baking a cake for Joe's birthday, even though it was still a few weeks away. She and the rest of the group stood in the hall and presented the chocolate cake with chocolate frosting and seventeen lit candles. Joe took one look and started jumping around and got so excited and loud that Alphonse threw open his apartment door and yelled, "Okay. Foutre le camp d'ici!" We got his drift. He had been looking to get rid of us since we showed up. Maybe Alphonse's displeasure had something to do with the fact that it was one in the morning. The icing on the cake.

The next morning, Alphonse allowed us to have a farewell breakfast with the group. Then me and Joe got our bikes and went out to the sidewalk in front of the Y to wait for my Uncle Ralph. All the kids and Belinda came out to say goodbye. They hugged us, slapped us on the back, thanked us, kissed our cheeks, wished us well, promised to get together for a reunion, and stuffed slips of paper with their phone numbers into our pockets. The girls cried.

I was especially sad to say goodbye to Gina. I never did tell her my real plan about running away. She hugged me, smiled, and told me, "You could get into your Dodge Coronet 440 and come to Sands Point. I can take you out sailing in my sailboat. I can't wait to introduce you to all my friends and my family. They'll just love you!"

The kids had often said that they had missed us when we were gone. Now, me and Joe realized that we were going to miss them. This was the end of the road for us and the group. In a few days, they would take a bus back to Springfield where their parents would pick them up. And, me and Joe would be at Aunt Bea's, planning our next move.

When Uncle Ralph drove up to the Y in his gigantic dark blue Pontiac Bonneville convertible with white leather seats, I thought, *wow!* for a couple of reasons. First, what a fucking car! It made my Dodge Coronet 440 look like a kiddie car. Second, I knew I would have to take the bikes apart to get them into the trunk of the Bonneville. Thank God it was a boat of a car.

This was the first time in six years that there had been any contact between my mother and the rest of her family. The estrangement was all the result of the fallout about which one of my mother's two sisters had been the one to call the New York state troopers to have my father arrested for supposedly stealing my dead Grampa's '64 gold Buick LeSabre. Another beautiful car. The really confusing part was that Aunt Fran, my mother's older sister who lived in Brooklyn, had actually been the one to place the call from her apartment in Brooklyn to the state troopers in Malone, New York, right near the Canadian border. But Aunt Fran had used Aunt Bea's name to place the call. Both aunts blamed each other for the call, and my mother didn't know whom to believe. Like I said, confusing.

Uncle Ralph gave us the grand tour of Montreal, like a couple of VIPs being escorted in his Bonneville convertible. The tour even included his butcher shop where he stopped in to make sure his workers weren't stealing from him. We finally made it to Aunt Bea's and Uncle Ralph's house in Chateauguay, a suburb of Montreal. It was a comfortable house in a safe suburban neighborhood, could have been Long Island or New Jersey or any suburb of any city really.

Aunt Bea and my cousins Mitch, Laurie, and Karen all came tumbling out the front door when we arrived, clapping and laughing and hugging us and yelling, "You made it! You made it! The boys from The Bronx really made it!" To them it must have been some kind of miracle. In a way, I guess it was. All the way from New York City, two sixteen-year-old kids, on bicycles, nearly four hundred miles all told. We hugged them back and were welcomed into their home.

One of the first things Aunt Bea told me, when she had the chance, was, "Steven, I hope you know I never called the state troopers on your father. It was all your Aunt Fran's idea. She used my name."

"Aunt Bea, you are my favorite aunt of all time. I never thought you would do that. But how about for now, let's just all be happy and be together and have a good time. And, by the way, I think my mom knows you didn't call."

Me and Joe were treated like royalty. Breakfast in bed, gourmet dinners, day trips, being shown off to all the cousins' friends and neighbors. I remember Aunt Bea even tried to fix me up with this cute little Israeli girl staying down the street for the summer. That's when I announced, "I have a girlfriend. Her name is Gina, but thanks anyway." That was the first time I thought of Gina in that way. As much as the Israeli girl was very pretty, I kept it all casual and kosher.

As the week with the relatives progressed, I felt like I had rediscovered some new old family. I loved my cousins, and my aunt and uncle regained their position as my favorites. We all vowed to let bygones be bygones and stay in touch. There were lots of telephone calls from Aunt Bea to my mother. I witnessed the two sisters laughing and crying and making up, promising to see each other real soon. That week in Montreal was a reunion of sorts. Everybody wanted to talk to each other and the phone was passed from one to the next. I spoke to my family a lot that week.

As the last day of the five-day visit approached, I mapped out an itinerary for our return trip and a plan for my exit. I figured I'd tell Joe somewhere in New Hampshire on our way down to Boston where our trip would end in a week or so. I planned on getting him a bus ticket home from Boston. I would be moving on. Alone.

On the last evening of our stay at Aunt Bea's, I called home one last time to say goodbye. As soon as I heard my mother's voice, I knew she had been crying. She begged me, "You have to come home. Soon. He's crazy. He's making life miserable for all of us. He's always drunk.

He hasn't worked for days. He says he can't work without you. Steve, we need you. Come back home." My heart sank. I had thought I was free. My gut wrenched, more for me than for my family. I had thought I was stronger. All it took for me to cave was hearing my mother cry.

It took us about a week to get to Boston. We got on the bus and marveled at how in four hours this bus could travel the distance it would take me and Joe a week to cover on our bikes.

I was sad but also relieved that I couldn't run away. Not yet. Besides, my extensive planning had only included getting us to Boston and saying goodbye to Joe. Beyond that, I had nothing.

Running away was something I had fixated on to try on the idea that I could want for something different, that I could get out in the world and be free. At least I knew I could bust out someday and I would. Maybe not today. But someday.

We got to Port Authority at Washington Heights, the same bus station where I orchestrated that Palisades trip for me and Elaine a few years earlier. We were back, we were home, we were tired, and we were proud. Me and Joe did the impossible. Six weeks on the road, somewhere around nine hundred miles. Joe had grown up and had become a celebrity. Me, I found a girl named Gina and a big, green world that I definitely would be getting back to someday.

We headed over the Washington Bridge into The Bronx and then north on University Avenue, east across

Fordham Road onto Pelham Parkway and then onto Allerton Avenue. It took about an hour to bike home. We were pros by then and this last leg was a piece of cake, especially after that restful bus ride.

Joe had notified everybody—meaning he had called Nicky from Port Authority who in turn told everybody—his friends, family, shopkeepers, all his people when we were going to arrive. I also had told my family. When we got to Allerton and Lurting Avenues, the whole block was lined with people, almost like a ticker-tape parade, all waving and screaming as we rode slowly up Allerton Avenue. We were heroes.

These people were all Joe's people. Yeah, I was the other half of the dynamic duo, but it was his mom, his dad, his brother, Joe's mother's sister, Sister Margaret, his neighbors, all his friends lining the street outside Vito's. I waved to everybody, told Joe I'd catch up to him later and rode down Lurting Avenue one block to my apartment. Nobody was home.

* * *

The day after we got back from our trip was a Friday. That weekend, just like Gina instructed me to, I took the Coronet 440 out to her house in Sands Point, Long Island. We did go sailing and her family did grow to love me.

That Monday, I went back to work at the plumbing shop. One of my main jobs was servicing a department store called May's in Brooklyn. They had a bunch of problems with their sinks and toilets and my old man told me to go out there and fix everything. When I got to the store, I realized it was going to be a few day's work and I would need some help to hand me tools and supplies and go back and forth from the van, in order to make the job go more efficiently. So I asked my old man if I could bring Joe with me. He thought that was a great idea since he really liked Joe and had nobody else he could spare to send with me.

Joe turned out to be a great assistant. I got the job done in two days because of his help. We had fun. I even taught him some basic toilet repairs. We gawked at girls shopping in the store. We rehashed every aspect of our trip, like the trip would last forever.

On the way home from Brooklyn on that second day, traffic was backed up on the FDR Drive all the way from Harlem to the Brooklyn Bridge. The night before, it hadn't been so bad and it still took us three hours. By rights, the trip should take no more than one hour. This night was looking to take at least five.

So, instead of pumping the clutch in the van for five hours, we decided to get off the highway and let the traffic die down while we took in some sights. As we pulled off the FDR Drive, west onto Pearl Street, we saw the two towers that were just being completed in the financial district. They were going to be the tallest buildings in the world. One hundred and ten stories each. You could see them from Brooklyn, New Jersey, and just about anywhere in Manhattan.

We drove a few blocks to Liberty Street and easily found a parking spot. It was 6:00 p.m., after the end of a work day. We had the streets to ourselves. The financial district was dead.

We got out, stretched our legs, and walked over to the towers. We looked up. And up. And up. We got dizzy. We couldn't see the top of either tower. Joe and I had never seen anything like it. He was in total awe. I shuddered.

Joe said, "Bernstein, imagine the science behind these things! Imagine how many toilets there are!" All of a sudden, from working with me a couple of days, he thought of himself as a toilet expert.

The towers scared me. Their magnitude. Their arrogance. Their purpose. America's sense of superiority. The World Trade Center. *America, center of the world.* And that awareness made me think of Vietnam. *What are we doing in Vietnam? Who or what are we trying to dominate in order for us, America, to be the center of the world? Why are we so important? Killing people overseas, building these giant towers, for what? Somehow the towers and Vietnam felt connected.*

Joe was all too eager to enlist as soon as he turned eighteen. Me? I had done a total 180 on enlisting after being accepted to the Air Force Academy and then seeing a high school buddy come home at eighteen with no legs.

His name was Freddy Schumacher. Me and Freddy were in the eleventh grade together at Clinton High

School. He was in my Spanish and trigonometry classes. He was failing both. One day, he came up to me at lunch and told me that unless he passed both classes, he was going to be left back again. He told me if that happened, he was going to drop out and enlist. Freddy was already eighteen and couldn't bear to be left back yet again.

Mrs. Mulligan, our Spanish teacher, was so upbeat and enthusiastic that she gave me a bunch of study materials to help pull Freddy's Spanish grade up to a D. Freddy couldn't even pronounce trigonometry, let alone do it. As hard as Freddy strained and as much as Mr. Edelstein, our trigonometry teacher, mentored me to tutor Freddy, he failed. Freddy dropped out and enlisted in the army.

The last time I saw Freddy was the day of my graduation from Clinton, held at the Loews Paradise movie theater on the Grand Concourse. At the end of the ceremony, the graduates strutted up the aisle to the theater exit, congratulating each other with handshakes, slaps on the back, wishing each other good luck.

On my way out, I saw Freddy in a wheelchair with his father standing behind him at the back of the theater. I was surprised to see him and then shocked when I saw that both of his legs were missing below the knees. I shook his outstretched hand. I had to stop myself from asking, "Howudoin'?" Freddy filled in the awkward quiet and said, "I thought I'd come up to see my friends graduate."

He congratulated me on being an honor student and in the same breath he said, "A twelve-year-old kid shot me in Nam."

In the same way that I hadn't known what to say to Freddy, I couldn't find the words to describe the feelings I had about these towers. I told Joe, "Yeah they are something, but why do we need them?"

"Lighten up, Bernstein, you think too much. This is the greatest feat of mankind to date. Show a little respect. America is on top of the world, look at these things!" I said nothing.

We stood there trying to take it all in, the cement, steel, and glass, the noisy crowded city, the heat, the traffic, all in contrast to the green and idyllic New England bike adventure we had just returned from and had been reliving, non-stop, for the last two days.

While everyone in New York, and perhaps even around the world, was gushing over these two structures, I had an eerily opposite reaction, one that I couldn't yet put into words. Instead of being impressed, I was depressed. My strong response, so different than my best buddy's standing right next to me, was triggered by these gigantic towers, Joe's unbridled enthusiasm and patriotism, along with the images of legless Freddy Schumacher, photos of Vietnamese napalm victims, and all the body bags coming home. Eventually, after one of my heroes, Muhammad Ali, said no to the war and refused to be drafted, I realized I, too, was becoming a pacifist.

Joe grabbed my hand in an exaggerated handshake and said, "Whatsamatta? You forgot today was my birthday? Bernstein, let's make a pact. Next year, when we turn eighteen, we go together to get our draft cards." Again, I said nothing.

* * *

Every year, for thirty years, from that day in the of summer 1971 when we were just a couple of kids in our own worlds with our own perspectives, looking up at those towers, Joe faithfully called me on his birthday to remind me to wish him a happy birthday. And then, a week later, he would wish me a happy birthday on mine.

So, over the many years, after I moved to New England, through two marriages, multiple contracting businesses, working with at-risk teens, being an animal rights activist, getting a bachelor's and then a master's degree in my forties, Amy's death at age forty-nine, through all of it, Joe and I stayed connected.

As for Joe, he stayed in New York. He became a bodybuilder and then a transit cop. Joe got married, had two kids, and moved to the suburbs. He realized his dream of becoming an Emergency Service cop, the most elite of all New York City police. He was stationed in Harlem. Jumpers, hostages, snipers, basically it was the SWAT team for the NYC police department.

Joe told me stories over the years about his work. A crack addict up in the Bronx holding his family hostage or a jumper off the Brooklyn Bridge. One time Joe called me because he needed my expertise about how to handle a reciprocating saw and what kind of blades to use to cut through some steel bars in order to save a toddler from certain death. Sometimes I worried about Joe, but he loved what he was doing, saving people.

Me and Joe saw each other once or twice every year, at least. We talked several times a year, especially on our birthdays. He brought his family up to the farm me and my second wife, Kate, had in New Hampshire where his kids got to meet all of the rescued animals. We gave the boys horsey rides and hot chocolate.

* * *

September 6, 2001, Gilsum, New Hampshire

The answering machine was recording Joe's birthday call: "Yo Bernstein! What the fuck? Pick up. Happy fuckin' birthday! Don't make me come up there, Bernstein, pick up the fuckin' phone, I wanna make sure you're still breathin'. . ."

It was good to hear his voice. I picked up the phone. "Hey man. You too. Sorry I'm late, as usual."

"No problem, buddy. What's shakin'? How you holdin' up? I'm so sorry about Amy, man, I know how close you two were. And you and Kate? Shit, man. What's next? Never mind."

STORIES FROM THE STOOP

I told him Cody died. "I loved that dog," I said.

"Fuck! Bernstein. Well, I hear it comes in threes. You gonna be all set now."

"Yeah, I hope so, I'm tired."

"You workin'? Kid stuff? Pipes? Animals? Whatchu up to?"

"Yeah, all of the above," I said. "Mostly kids. I got the non-profit funded and good programs in place. I'm liking it, but, honestly I lost my mojo."

"It'll come back," Joe said.

"Yeah."

"So, how 'bout you? Nancy and the kids good?"

"Everyone's great. They're always asking if they can come up and ride the horses again. I gotta figure out a way to tell them about divorce, I guess. I'll leave that to Nancy."

"Tell me a work story, I love that shit," I said.

"I don't know man. It's fuckin' weird down here. It's like tense. Nothing really out of the ordinary other than some chatter about terrorism."

"Terrorism? What do you mean?" I was thinking terrorism in Israel, El Salvador, Lebanon, Spain.

"Yeah, something about terrorists. I got nothing else. It's weird." I was thinking at least it's not the run of the mill axe murderers and child abductors and bridge jumpers, that's the shit that got me scared for Joe. Terrorists? Here in the US? Terrorists blew up things in other countries. Not here. Very strange.

We talked for over an hour. Warm. Caring. Close. Closer than ever before. "How are the folks?" I asked.

"Good, my dad is getting old, turned eighty-eight last month, my mom still spry as ever."

"Give them my love"

"I will, man."

"So whaddya think about my idea I ran by you last time we talked?" he asked.

I had to think for a minute. "Oh the memorial bike ride! Yeah, it's thirty years, wow! You still know how?" I asked.

"Fuck you, Bernstein."

"It's a good time of year, I'm in."

"Yeah, I gotta get a bike though."

"Some things never change," I said.

"Fuck you, Bernstein."

"I got some time off in a couple weeks, let's really do this," he said.

"I got an extra bike, don't sweat it."

"No Canada this time. It's not the distance, I just don't wanna see you get all the girls again," he whined. "You hear from Gina?"

"Naw, never stayed in touch."

"Wonder how she's doin'," he said. "You know if you want to, I could track her down. I got resources."

"Great idea man. I miss her." I said.

"Gotta go. Talk soon. Let's fuckin' do this bike trip. I love you, man."

Then I did something that I had never done before. Joe always ended our talks with "I love you, man." Before we hung up, I said, "Me too, Joe. Please be careful."

That was my birthday. September 6, 2001. I had just turned forty-seven. Five days later, I was scheduled to do a presentation about my work with kids at Keene State College. It was a perfect day. Late summer, clear blue sky, mid-seventies, just a gorgeous day.

I had temporary custody of Libby, a coyote-dog mix, who Kate and I had adopted together years before. If Libby turned out to be happy with me, Kate and I had agreed that I would keep her permanently. Libby was very timid but so sweet. Though she missed her buddies back home with Kate, all signs were looking good that she and I were hitting it off together in our new life.

After a beautiful morning hike in the woods with Libby, at about 9:45, I strolled into the Student Center at Keene State, looking for Matt and the rest of my staff to get ready for our 10:00 a.m. presentation. Matt was a good friend from Antioch University graduate school whom I had hired to be a program director in my organization.

Strangely, the vast hall was quiet. The only noise was the sound of the four TVs suspended from the ceiling. Clusters of students, along with my staff, were staring up at the screens, mesmerized. Occasionally one gasped.

"You don't know, do you?" Matt asked me.

"Know what? Me and Libby were out in the woods hiking." Thinking I had arrived late, I asked, "The talk was supposed to be at 10:00, right?"

Matt pushed me in front of one of the TVs and said, "New York, the Twin Towers, the planes. Here, look." I saw recordings of a plane hitting the North Tower and then a second plane hitting the South Tower. Silently we watched as these images played over and over again.

At 9:59 the four screens switched to live footage. We shrieked as the South Tower collapsed in front of our eyes.

The chaos on the screen, the chaos in that hall, all faded away. I pointed to the TV screen, and shouted, "Joe is in there. Joe is in that building!" I knew he was in there saving people. That's what he did, what he loved.

At that moment, all I knew is that my buddy had just blown up, disintegrated, extinguished.

Those were the same towers we had gawked at when they were brand new, thirty years before almost to the day, when we were just a couple of kids. Joe had been all excited and proud to be an American that day. And I had a bad feeling about those buildings.

I waited two days until I called Nancy, Joe's wife. I got her sister who was there watching the boys. She confirmed that Joe had been in one of the buildings.

The following day, I got a call from Nicky, Joe's twin brother. All he could say was, "I hate those fucking Muslims, I want to kill all of them!"

I just listened and let him have his grief. I gave Nicky my condolences and asked if I could come down to the city. He said, "Yeah, that's what I was calling you about. Joe would want you here."

A week later on September 18 I got down to Joe's house and stayed with Nancy and the kids. Every day the families, spouses mainly, went down to One Police Plaza, the main police headquarters and the hub of police oversight for the attack. Loved ones arrived at the building every morning, and waited to be told the status of their loved ones. The victims were considered missing, not officially dead until body parts, tissue, or DNA had been found.

It seemed like torture to me. They were all dead. All gone. After the first day, no one had been pulled out alive. No more survivors.

After watching the kids a few days while Nancy spent all day at One Police Plaza, Mary, Joe's mom, called the house. She told me, "Joey thought of you as family. Go down to One Police Plaza with the rest of them. The officers will take you to the site and show you where Joey was last seen. It will be good for you," she said.

The next day, on my way down to One Police Plaza, I stopped at Joe's parents' house in The Bronx to pay my respects. We couldn't remember the last time we had seen each other. It must have been when I lived down the block, thirty years earlier. Mary and her husband, Joe Sr., now quite old but still very sharp, were as gracious and kind as they always had been.

The house was exactly as I had remembered it in 1971 only today the curtains were drawn and the living room smelled of flowers. On every table, bookcase, and mantel were displayed giant bouquets of flowers—lilies, irises, orchids, and white roses.

Condolence cards and rosary beads were laid out on the mantel, next to a picture of Joe in his ESU uniform, a grappling rope wound around his shoulder with a big smile, ear-to-ear, the Brooklyn Bridge in the background. I remember the story he told me that day. He had rescued a jumper, climbed up the Brooklyn Bridge, and got him down. He loved saving people.

Tears running down his cheeks, Joe Sr. stammered, "Those planes, those buildings. Joey was going to retire this year. He had his twenty years in. Why? Why?" Mary put her hand on his shoulder and then wiped away his tears with the sleeve of her housecoat.

Mary took me to the kitchen where she had laid out tuna fish sandwiches and coffee. She said, "I don't know if you really knew how much Joey loved you, looked up to you as a brother. He never stopped talking about you, even recently. What are you up to? Rescuing crazy teenagers and going vegan? You're still a plumber aren't you?"

"Always."

"Good, don't give that up, it's good money." Mary told me how I had helped Joe figure out that he wanted to be a cop. "I wish now you didn't help him, but that's what my Joey wanted more than anything. Nothing would have stopped him, he wanted to save people. He always wanted to save you, you know. But, I told him you didn't need saving. I told him the best thing he could do is just be your friend."

"He was always that, he never gave up on me."

"I know you two were going to do another ride soon. Too bad. That woulda been good for Joey. The job was getting to him and he only had six months to go."

Mary started crying and I hugged her. Tears were pouring out now, both of us. Mary said, "Now Steve, get down to the station, they'll take you to the site. It will do you good to see it. It's crazy, what do they think they're gonna find? Joey and all the rest of them are dead, gone. It's just a pile of smoking garbage now. Tell them to stop torturing us, going down there, waiting. Waiting, for what? A finger? A foot? Stop already, they're dead! Go!" I hugged Mary one last time and shook Joe Sr.'s hand. I took off downtown.

Up in The Bronx, it was strangely quiet. Traffic was light. Not many people on the street. So different than what I remembered driving in the city to be. It was a breeze.

I took the Bronx River Parkway to the Sheridan Expressway to the Bruckner Expressway to the FDR. After the Manhattan Bridge, everything changed. There was no way I would be able to continue driving to One Police Plaza. It was a war zone. Barricades, National Guard, and cops everywhere. Traffic was diverted away from the police station so I had to park in Chinatown. I grabbed a bowl of soup and then headed south on Mott Street. At Canal Street, then again at Worth Street, I was asked to identify myself by National Guard troops, dressed in full body armor, carrying assault rifles. I told them that I was a close friend to one of the ESU cops killed on 9/11, and that I would be allowed on Ground Zero as part of the family. At Pearl Street, the final barricaded intersection, I was again asked to identify myself. A gruff, no-nonsense ESU cop looked at my driver's license and said, "You ain't no family member. You're gonna have to leave. Please turn around."

"Yeah, but I just came from my buddy's parents and they told me I was on the list, that all I had to do was see the commanding officer at PP1 and they would take me to Ground Zero."

The cop examined my license again, and then looked back at me and said "New Hampshire?" He thought a moment, "Steve?" And then, he thought another moment and asked, "You a plumber?"

"Yeah."

A big smile came over his face as he pulled off his helmet, put down his gun, and hugged me tight up against his bulletproof vest. "Joey loved you man, he was always talking about you. Wow, that bike trip the two of you's took as kids, that was sumthin', huh?" he said. Tears were flowing from both our eyes. Then he said, "He was the best, that Joey was."

"I know," I said, "I know."

"You're all set man, go ahead up, it's down the block to the right. And oh, by the way, thanks for telling Joey what blades to use that day when he called you. We saved that little kid."

I got to One Police Plaza which was essentially being used as a clearing house for relatives to come and wait and maybe be taken to Ground Zero, or maybe be given some information about a loved one's status, like some thing or some body part was found and the cops could officially move them from the missing list to the dead list.

I made it through the crowd and checked in. My name was on the list as a family member.

I saw Nicky, Nancy, and her sister. He ran up to me and shook my hand and told me Joe would have wanted me to be part of this. Nicky was a little buzzed and kept saying, "I want all those fucking Muslims dead." His tone, the attitude brought me back to their neighborhood in the North Bronx in 1971: "Spics this and the niggers that. Get them the fuck outta here. They don't belong." I wasn't about to start a lecture about how the attack wasn't representative of Islam; these were psychopaths. But I sure wanted to. Understandably, he had nowhere to go with his rage at losing his twin brother. Makes sense that he would turn to blame and hate.

Later that day, Nicky and Nancy left One Police Plaza as there was no information about Joe. No pieces or parts or guts or DNA. He was still considered missing.

The place started emptying out at around eight that night when mostly everyone was told their loved ones were still missing. The sergeant on duty came over to me several times and assured me I would get an escort into Ground Zero soon. His shift ended and the next sergeant came over at about eleven and told me the same thing.

I kept saying, "No problem, I'm fine, don't worry about me." I didn't want to be a burden. The cops were all so gracious and polite and trying to make it right for everybody under the gravest of circumstances.

By midnight I had fallen asleep, my head resting on a wooden table. An officer came over, tapped me on the back, and asked if I was ready to go. I had been waiting about nine hours and was very tired, but I perked right up and said, "Absolutely, thank you so much."

She and the sergeant personally drove me over to the Ground Zero site. The short ride was eerie, there was no traffic except for military and police vehicles. New York would never be the same for me after this.

The cops led me into the lobby of a building right near Ground Zero, I think on Vesey or maybe Liberty Street. I don't remember. The windows and doors were blown out and the place was buzzing with hundreds of rescue workers. It was the temporary command center. There were maps and charts on the walls and walkie-talkies and two-way radios blaring. My official escorts introduced me as Joe's best friend and asked if I would be able to see the site. The officer on duty shook my hand, looked me in the eye, and told me, "Joey was my partner. He was the best, he was saving lives when the fucking tower collapsed." He handed me a gas mask and brought me out to Ground Zero. He said, "We don't call this Ground Zero, we call it The Pile." I saw why.

It was dark. I felt the ground shaking. I saw plumes of smoke and an occasional flare up of fire. Gigantic glaring lights were set up everywhere, and an unidentifiable stench filled the air. Construction crews with monstrous digging machines—like I had never seen before in all my years working construction—were chipping away at piles of debris, eight or ten stories tall. Every time their claws hit the pile, smoke would discharge and fire would flare up.

Joe's partner was very polite and respectful to me. He pointed to the largest pile of rubble and said, "That's where I saw him last. He was taking people out of the building right there where there used to be a mezzanine. I was the last guy to see him." I stood staring at the place he indicated. He left me alone and told me to come back to the command center whenever I was ready, but to make sure to keep the gas mask on. "This shit will kill you if you breathe too much in," he told me.

As the giant machine pounced, the ground shook. The fog of fumes and night mist and dust, the giant lights, the piles of debris being attacked, big trucks rolling by, people with gas masks scurrying around an area the size of fifteen football fields made me feel like I was on a different planet. The machines seemed like fire-breathing monsters and the people with the gas masks seemed like aliens. Standing on a mound of smoking pulverized rubble, maybe twenty-five feet in the air, I just took it all in. And then, for several minutes, my eyes fixated on the spot where Joe had been last seen. I gazed up beyond the glare and smoke and noise and said a prayer for my friend. And the rest of us as well.

I stayed in the city a few more days, helping Nancy with the kids and then headed back home to New Hampshire. After all, Libby was waiting for me and I had an organization to run, staff and teens counting on me.

After bouncing around following my separation from my second wife, home now was a tiny cabin up on a mountain in the southwestern part of the state. It was good to be on solid ground.

I was ready to get on with my life. Amy had been sick for years and, after a long battle with ovarian cancer, had finally passed away not too long before 9/11. Years earlier I had helped my father get off the streets of The Bronx, where he had been homeless. I moved him to a veterans home where, for the rest of his life, he was safe. My brother and mother had also escaped The Bronx and ended up living in Amherst, Massachusetts. She had kept that one postcard I had sent her of Amherst from the bike trip. That postcard motivated her to take Richard and leave the city.

About a month after I got back from Ground Zero, late October, I got the call from Nicky that there was going to be a funeral. After all that waiting, Joe's DNA was located and identified. Joe was no longer missing. He was officially dead.

Nancy invited me to stay with her and the kids, but had to warn me that the two boys, aged three and eight, still didn't understand. And also, she asked, "Please don't tell them about you and your wife, they got enough to deal with, they wouldn't understand divorce. They keep asking when they can go up and ride the horses again."

Joe's funeral was in a giant stone church in their town just outside the city. The place was packed with cops and firefighters and dignitaries and all Joe's family and friends from back in the day. It felt like nobody had aged, like we were all kids again. They all knew each other well. There I was, Joe's friend, the outsider.

At the service, several people came up to the altar and spoke about how they knew Joe. Some cops talked about his bravery and his stupid jokes. A few of his old friends talked about how he had been the sane one, the nice one, the levelheaded one of the crowd.

Dominic, Joe's oldest friend from way back before kindergarten, delivered the main eulogy. A sweet guy. I knew him a little bit and always liked him. Dominic talked about Joe and the mischief they got into and how great a dad Joe was and how great a man he was. Then he said, "One summer, it was the craziest thing. Joe had a friend named Steve and they took a bike trip all the way up to Canada and back. When Joe came home from that trip, he was different. He seemed wiser, older, happier. Joe told me it was the best thing he ever did." Dominic went on about how much he loved Joe. And why.

The service ended. I said goodbye to everybody, knowing most likely I would never see them again.

When I got back to my little cabin, I slept a few days straight. I kept the news off. I didn't answer the phone. My staff tried to reach me several times. Matt even came up to the house looking for me.

The one thing I said yes to in those days following Joe's funeral was giving a homily about 9/11 at the Unitarian church in Manchester, New Hampshire. I agreed to speak, even though I wasn't sure I had anything to say. And then I realized that I did have something to say. I didn't know why 9/11 happened. I didn't have a clue about what's getting into us as human beings on this planet. But, for me, my experience of 9/11 was about love and connection. I told the congregation about my friend Joe. I told them how he never gave up on our friendship. I told them about our bike trip. I told them about his family. I told them about my journey down to Ground Zero in September.

I focused on love, not hate. I shared with the congregation about the mosque across the street from the North Bronx apartment where I was staying when I visited Ground Zero. The street outside the mosque was lined with police cruisers. These NYC cops were guarding the mosque from hate mongers, some of whom did more than just talk. I stopped and spoke to a Muslim man in front of the mosque. When I asked him how he was doing, he responded, "Me and my family are very afraid. We have already received threats." As we parted, we shook hands and I said, "*Shalom Aleichem*," Hebrew for "peace be with you." And he responded in kind, "*Wa alaikum assalaam*," Arabic for "and peace unto you." As New Yorkers and Semites, we understood these traditional greetings perfectly, even though we spoke them in different languages.

I shared with the congregation a promise I had made to myself: Tomorrow is never a guarantee. I promise to be there for the ones I love. I promise to always cherish the time we have together in this life. God knows, it's so short. I asked the congregation to do the same.

That Monday following my Sunday talk at the Unitarian church, I felt better. Clearer. I was relieved to have figured out what 9/11 meant to me. I joyfully thought about my friendship with Joe and lamented our thirty-year anniversary bike ride that we never got to do.

That October afternoon, I walked over to my shed where I kept some garden tools and a pile of obsolete, very heavy old tools that my old man insisted I take before he went into the veterans home years ago. I kept lugging that shit around everywhere I went, not sure why I didn't just scrap them.

Behind that crap were two Schwinns. One was a rusted Schwinn Suburban which was the replacement bike after my Continental was stolen back in The Bronx. The very same classic Continental with the chrome fork that I rode up to Canada on that trip with Joe so long ago. The other bike in the shed was a Schwinn Sierra. Not so great. Flimsy. Schwinn wasn't what it used to be. This was called a hybrid bike. Something between road and mountain. I didn't really need two bikes, but Raymond, one of the young men in my program, was about to be arrested. He came to me desperate and scared one night. Ray had done something really, really bad. He knew he was going away for a long time and he was worried about his two-year-old daughter. Ray asked if I could buy the Schwinn Sierra from him so he could give the money to the baby's mom while he was gone.

The Sierra was in good shape. The Suburban not so much. I took the Sierra out of the shed, cleaned it up, put some air in the tires, and rode it down my quarter-mile-long dirt driveway. When I hit the road, I banged a right and rode along the Ashuelot River like I was sixteen and it was 1971. I felt Amy and Joe right there with me.

A few miles down I saw a handmade sign on my neighbor's mailbox. It said Free Kittens. I knocked on the door and a woman introduced me first to the mother cat named Belle and then to her six babies.

Right away, this black and white tuxedo kitten came up to me and meowed and rubbed on me and rolled over on his back, showed me his belly, and clowned around with his siblings. He was very cute, but loud and a little obnoxious. And right then he looked up at me, right into my eyes, and let out a long yowl. It almost sounded like, "Yo, Bernstein." I named him Joey.

I rode back home, scooped Libby up, got in my truck, went into town, and bought a whole bunch of kitty things: a cat box, a yellow breakaway collar with one of those little metal name tags that said, "I belong to Steve Bernstein," some toys, a cat carrier, a little brush, a packet of catnip, and some organic top-of-the-line cat food. On the way home I stopped back at the neighbor's and put Joey, now fussing and yowling, into the carrier and went home. My new family was growing. After a few weeks I found Joey a sister. Her name was Frankie, a beautiful sweet, moon-faced grey tiger kitty.

The day I adopted Joey was one of those glorious New England fall days when the sun was strong, peaking through the lush leaves, birds happily sang, a warm breeze wafted by, the sky was bright blue, and the air was clean and fresh. It was almost impossible to be in a foul mood. I sat on the steps of my porch and felt myself basking in gratitude. How could I not? I'm here. I made it. I got life. I'm going to keep going.

My wooden steps felt like a stoop. So what if they weren't granite, cold and hard? It's okay if there was no chaos and craziness around me. No cars on the street, no kids playing stick ball or skipping rope Double Dutch. No moms calling out the windows for their kids to come in for dinner. No junkies. No drunkenness. No congas.

No salsa music. Nobody fighting or screaming. No soot in the air. No street sweeper trucks swishing dog shit around. No sirens blaring. No gangs or gang fights.

Amy's gone. Joe's gone. Half my life is gone. But I'm at peace. Open to the next adventure.